NINJA FOODI 2-BASKET

AIR FRYER

COOKBOOK

FOR BEGINNERS

CRISPY ,TASTY AND DELICIOUS RECIPES FOR EASY AND HEALTHY MEALS

KENNETH CROSBY

CONTENTS

INTRODUCTION

How do Ninja Foodi 2-Basket Air Fryer Works?

Air fryers work by circulating hot air around the food in a very similar way to convection ovens. A heating element inside the air fryer distributes hot air through a fan so that it's pushed around the food in circular motions. This way of cooking food is actually quicker than traditional methods because the heat is evenly distributed around the food. If you're cooking frozen fries in an air fryer, you can expect this to take around 15 minutes.

While air-frying might not be quite as fast as deep-frying, you'll be using significantly less oil, and you won't need to blot your food onto a paper kitchen towel. Most air fryers have removable baskets in which you place your food, and these have small holes all around their edges that allow the hot air to reach the food inside. In order for the air to circulate effectively though, you'll need to make sure you're not overfilling the basket so that the hot air can reach all sides of the food. Air fryer baskets sit pretty snugly against the sides of the appliance, ensuring that minimal heat is lost during cooking.

What Are the Benefits of Ninja Foodi 2-Basket Air Fryer?

I'm sure you have seen the online buzz about air fryers! These appliances are definitely the most popular and trendy thing happening in the kitchen this year. Maybe you are curious about what all the hype is about? When I first heard about them, I was curious as well. Why ARE people so excited about these things? I love some good fries as much as the next person, but can one unit really do more than that? How can frying anything be healthy?

These appliances are not a fryer in the same way that a deep-fat fryer is. They are more like a small, self-contained convection oven. They use electrical elements to quickly heat the air, and then circulate this hot air around and through your food. This hot air cooks the food quickly, so crispy things get browned but the inside stays moist and delicious. Here are some benefits of cooking with an air fryer:

1. Healthier Cooking

So, how can frying something be healthy? Easy! These appliances can be used without any oil at all, or with just a tiny spritz of oil if you choose to use it. You can cook frozen fries, onion rings, wings and more, and still get really crispy results without the extra oil. Compared to using my oven, the fries from the air fryer were crispier but not dried out, and using it to make breaded zucchini wedges was even more impressive!

2. Quicker Meals

Since they are smaller than an oven and circulate the air around with fans, they cook foods faster as well. An oven can take up to 20-30 minutes to properly preheat, whereas these fryers come to the temperature within minutes. I was really impressed that my frozen fries were perfect after 15 minutes when they take up to 45 minutes in the oven. If you need to make snacks or meals in a hurry, you will probably love this time saver.

3. Versatility

I think this is my favorite feature of an air fryer. You can do SO MUCH with it! Yes, it fries really well compared to an oven. But it also can bake (even cakes), broil, roast, grill and stir fry! Feel like chicken and snow peas for dinner? Easy to make with one of these.

You can cook fresh and frozen foods and even reheat leftovers in them. I have done meats, fish, casseroles, sandwiches and a lot of different veggies in mine. Some fryers come with extra features, like a rotisserie rack, grill pan or elevated cooking rack. Dividable baskets mean you can cook several things at the same time as well. It is impressive that a single unit can cook so many things in so many ways.

Depending on the size of your fryer, there are a lot of different accessories you can buy. Cake and pizza pans, kabob skewers and steamer inserts are just a few of the accessories I have seen available. There are many recipe books for sale, and online recipes are easy to find too.

4. Space Saver

If you have a small kitchen, or live in a dorm room or shared housing, you might appreciate this benefit. Most of these units are about the size of a coffee maker. They don't take up too much room on the counter, and they are usually easy to store away or move. I appreciate the fact that they can replace other appliances like a toaster oven, and some folks use them in kitchenettes or RVs that lack a real oven. They are very handy to have in an office break room too!

5. Ease of Use

Most fryers are really easy to use- just select the temperature and the cooking time, add food and shake a few times while cooking. No need to fuss or stir like using the stove top.

The baskets make shaking your food simple and fast as well, and the unit doesn't lose a lot of heat when you open it. So feel free to peek while cooking if you want! Unlike an oven, you won't be slowing things down if you do.

6. Ease of Clean Up

One part of cooking that most of us don't enjoy is the clean up. With an air fryer, you just have a basket and pan to clean, and many are even dishwasher safe. With non-stick coated parts, food usually isn't stuck to the pan and instead slides right off onto your plate. It takes just a few minutes to wash up after using. This inspires me to cook at home more often because I don't dread the clean up!

7. Energy Efficiency

These fryers are more efficient that using an oven, and they won't heat up you house either. I've been using mine during a heat wave, and I love that my kitchen isn't hot while I'm using it. If you are trying to keep your house cool during the summer, or are worried about your electric bill, then you will be impressed with how efficient these units are.

How to Use Ninja Foodi 2-Basket Air Fryer?

Here are a few more tips for getting the most out of your air fryer:

1. Adjust the Cooking Temperature

When converting a recipe with a suggested temperature for deep-frying or cooking in a traditional oven, lower the air fryer's temperature by 25°F to achieve similar results. So if a recipe calls for deep-frying chicken in oil heated to 350°F, air fry at 325°F. The same rule applies for converting roasting recipes. This adjustment is needed because the circulating air makes the heat of the cooking environment more consistent, and thus more intense than traditional cooking methods. Remember to pre-heat your air fryer to temperature—it usually takes less than 5 minutes—before filling the basket, just as you would with any other cooking method.

2. Toss Ingredients With Oil, Sparingly

In general, you should toss food with one to two tablespoons of oil (whichever kind you like: olive, coconut, canola). Foods that are naturally fattier, like meatballs, needn't be tossed in any additional oil. For foods that have been battered or dredged in flour, we recommend spraying the air fryer basket or rack first with cooking spray, laying your battered or dredged food in the basket or rack in a single layer, and then giving the food a light spritz of cooking spray just to coat the top. That little bit of oil is essential for getting foods to turn golden-brown, crisp, and appealing.

3. Fill the Air Fryer Basket or Rack

Battered and floured foods should be placed in one layer in an air fryer basket or rack. Some models offer racks that allow for two layers—if yours does, feel free to double up. For things like French fries or "roasted" vegetables, you can load the air fryer basket to the top; however, a fuller basket will require a longer cooking time and will result in food that's not quite as crisp as a basket with a smaller amount of food. It's also a good idea to give full baskets a shake every 3 to 5 minutes to make sure food is cooking evenly—many models will pause the timer when you open the drawer, expressly for this purpose.

4. Check for Doneness Early

Again, because the circulating air helps the air-fryer cooking environment maintain a more consistent temperature than other cooking methods, foods tend to cook faster in an air fryer than they do when being deep-fried or cooked in a conventional oven. That means if you're converting a recipe you already know and love to one cooked in an air fryer, you'll want to check the food about two-thirds of the way through the suggested cooking time to test doneness. Those fish sticks say they'll be done in 15 minutes? Check them at 10 minutes.

5. Make French Fries as Often as Possible

We know why you're really thinking about buying that air fryer, so here it is: yup, frozen French fries can be put right into the air fryer, no oil necessary, and cooked at 350°F for about 15 minutes. Be sure to give them a shake or a toss once or twice during cooking. Fresh-cut fries should first be soaked in hot water for at least 10 minutes (30 minutes is better) to remove excess starch. After soaking, drain and dry fries with a kitchen towel, toss in 1 to 2 tablespoons vegetable oil, then air fry at 350°F for about 20 minutes, again shaking once or twice during cooking. And in either case, don't forget to salt them when they're finished cooking.

How to Clean and Care for Ninja Foodi 2-Basket Air Fryer?

Traditionally, deep frying food is very messy. You end up with a lot of dirty pans, grimy utensils, and a greasy coating on everything around the fryer. Air fryers, on the other hand, are relatively clean. The cooking basket is completely enclosed, which eliminates splattering and all the fat, grease, and oil in your food drips down into the oil pan below. This doesn't mean there's no need to clean, however. Your air fryer should be cleaned every time you use it.

➢ **To clean your Ninja Foodi 2-Basket air fryer:**

✧ Unplug the air fryer from the wall socket and let it cool down.

✧ Wipe the outside with a damp cloth.

✧ Wash the pan, tray, and basket with hot water and dishwashing soap. All the air fryer's removable components are dishwasher safe, so they can be placed in a dishwasher if you would prefer not to wash them by hand.

✧ Clean in the inside of the air fryer with hot water and a cloth or sponge.

✧ If there is any food stuck to the heating element above the food basket, clean it off with a brush.

✧ Make sure the pan, tray, and basket are completely dry before putting them back into the air fryer.

➢ **To care your Ninja Foodi 2-Basket air fryer:**

Beyond regularly cleanings, your air fryer requires some basic maintenance to make sure that it doesn't get damaged or start functioning incorrectly. This includes:

✧ Inspecting the cords before each use. Never plug a damaged or frayed cord into an outlet. It can cause serious injury or even death. Make sure the cords are clean and damage-free before using your air fryer.

✧ Making sure the unit is clean and free of any debris before you start cooking. If it has been a long time since you last used your air fryer, check inside. Some dust may have accumulated. If there is any food residue on the basket for pan, clean it out before you start cooking.

✧ Make sure the air fryer is placed upright, on a level surface, before you start cooking.

✧ Make sure the air fryer is not placed close to a wall or another appliance. Air fryers need at least 4 inches of space behind them and 4 inches of space above them in order to adequately vent steam and hot air while cooking. Placing them in an enclosed space may cause the fryer to overheat.

✧ Visually inspect each component, including the basket, pan and handle prior to each use. If you find any damaged components, contact the manufacturer and get them replaced.

BREAD AND BREAKFAST

Banana Bread

Servings: 6

Cooking Time: 20 Minutes

Ingredients:

➢ cooking spray
➢ 1 cup white wheat flour
➢ ½ teaspoon baking powder
➢ ¼ teaspoon salt
➢ ¼ teaspoon baking soda
➢ 1 egg
➢ ½ cup mashed ripe banana
➢ ¼ cup plain yogurt
➢ ¼ cup pure maple syrup
➢ 2 tablespoons coconut oil
➢ ½ teaspoon pure vanilla extract

Directions:

1. Preheat air fryer to 330°F.

2. Lightly spray 6 x 6-inch baking dish with cooking spray.

3. In a medium bowl, mix together the flour, baking powder, salt, and soda.

4. In a separate bowl, beat the egg and add the mashed banana, yogurt, syrup, oil, and vanilla. Mix until well combined.

5. Pour liquid mixture into dry ingredients and stir gently to blend. Do not beat. Batter may be slightly lumpy.

6. Pour batter into baking dish and cook at 330°F for 20 minutes or until toothpick inserted in center of loaf comes out clean.

Blueberry Muffins

Servings: 8

Cooking Time: 14 Minutes

Ingredients:

- 1⅓ cups flour
- ½ cup sugar
- 2 teaspoons baking powder
- ¼ teaspoon salt
- ⅓ cup canola oil
- 1 egg
- ½ cup milk
- ⅔ cup blueberries, fresh or frozen and thawed
- 8 foil muffin cups including paper liners

Directions:

1. Preheat air fryer to 330°F.
2. In a medium bowl, stir together flour, sugar, baking powder, and salt.
3. In a separate bowl, combine oil, egg, and milk and mix well.
4. Add egg mixture to dry ingredients and stir just until moistened.
5. Gently stir in blueberries.
6. Spoon batter evenly into muffin cups.
7. Place 4 muffin cups in air fryer basket and bake at 330°F for 14 minutes or until tops spring back when touched lightly.
8. Repeat previous step to cook remaining muffins.

Breakfast Pot Pies

Servings: 4

Cooking Time: 20 Minutes

Ingredients:

- 1 refrigerated pie crust
- ½ pound pork breakfast sausage
- ¼ cup diced onion
- 1 garlic clove, minced
- ½ teaspoon ground black pepper
- ¼ teaspoon salt
- 1 cup chopped bell peppers
- 1 cup roasted potatoes
- 2 cups milk
- 2 to 3 tablespoons all-purpose flour

Directions:

1. Flatten the store-bought pie crust out on an even surface. Cut 4 equal circles that are slightly larger than the circumference of ramekins (by about ¼ inch). Set aside.

2. In a medium pot, sauté the breakfast sausage with the onion, garlic, black pepper, and salt. When browned, add in the bell peppers and potatoes and cook an additional 3 to 4 minutes to soften the bell peppers. Remove from the heat and portion equally into the ramekins.

3. To the same pot (without washing it), add the milk. Heat over medium-high heat until boiling. Slowly reduce to a simmer and stir in the flour, 1 tablespoon at a time, until the gravy thickens and coats the back of a wooden spoon (about 5 minutes).

4. Remove from the heat and equally portion ½ cup of gravy into each ramekin on top of the sausage and potato mixture.

5. Place the circle pie crusts on top of the ramekins, lightly pressing them down on the perimeter of each ramekin with the prongs of a fork. Gently poke the prongs into the center top of the pie crust a few times to create holes for the steam to escape as the pie cooks.

6. Bake in the air fryer for 6 minutes (or until the tops are golden brown).

7. Remove and let cool 5 minutes before serving.

Almond Cranberry Granola

Servings: 12

Cooking Time: 9 Minutes

Ingredients:

➢ 2 tablespoons sesame seeds

➢ ¼ cup chopped almonds

➢ ¼ cup sunflower seeds

➢ ½ cup unsweetened shredded coconut

➢ 2 tablespoons unsalted butter, melted or at least softened

➢ 2 tablespoons coconut oil

➢ ⅓ cup honey

➢ 2½ cups oats

➢ ¼ teaspoon sea salt

➢ ½ cup dried cranberries

Directions:

1. In a large mixing bowl, stir together the sesame seeds, almonds, sunflower seeds, coconut, butter, coconut oil, honey, oats, and salt.

2. Line the air fryer basket with parchment paper. Punch 8 to 10 holes into the parchment paper with a fork so air can circulate. Pour the granola mixture onto the parchment paper.

3. Air fry the granola at 350°F for 9 minutes, stirring every 3 minutes.

4. When cooking is complete, stir in the dried cranberries and allow the mixture to cool. Store in an airtight container up to 2 weeks or freeze for 6 months.

Goat Cheese, Beet, And Kale Frittata

Servings: 6

Cooking Time: 20 Minutes

Ingredients:

➢ 6 large eggs

➢ ½ teaspoon garlic powder

➢ ¼ teaspoon black pepper

➢ ¼ teaspoon salt

➢ 1 cup chopped kale

➢ 1 cup cooked and chopped red beets

➢ ⅓ cup crumbled goat cheese

Directions:

1. Preheat the air fryer to 320°F.

2. In a medium bowl, whisk the eggs with the garlic powder, pepper, and salt. Mix in the kale, beets, and goat cheese.

3. Spray an oven-safe 7-inch springform pan with cooking spray. Pour the egg mixture into the pan and place it in the air fryer basket.

4. Cook for 20 minutes, or until the internal temperature reaches 145°F.

5. When the frittata is cooked, let it set for 5 minutes before removing from the pan.

6. Slice and serve immediately.

Pigs In A Blanket

Servings: 10

Cooking Time: 8 Minutes

Ingredients:

- ➤ 1 cup all-purpose flour, plus more for rolling
- ➤ 1 teaspoon baking powder
- ➤ ¼ cup salted butter, cut into small pieces
- ➤ ½ cup buttermilk
- ➤ 10 fully cooked breakfast sausage links

Directions:

1. In a large mixing bowl, whisk together the flour and baking powder. Using your fingers or a pastry blender, cut in the butter until you have small pea-size crumbles.

2. Using a rubber spatula, make a well in the center of the flour mixture. Pour the buttermilk into the well, and fold the mixture together until you form a dough ball.

3. Place the sticky dough onto a floured surface and, using a floured rolling pin, roll out until ½-inch thick. Using a round biscuit cutter, cut out 10 rounds, reshaping the dough and rolling out, as needed.

4. Place 1 fully cooked breakfast sausage link on the left edge of each biscuit and roll up, leaving the ends slightly exposed.

5. Using a pastry brush, brush the biscuits with the whisked eggs, and spray them with cooking spray.

6. Place the pigs in a blanket into the air fryer basket with at least 1 inch between each biscuit. Set the air fryer to 340°F and cook for 8 minutes.

Fried Pb&j

Servings: 4

Cooking Time: 8 Minutes

Ingredients:

- ½ cup cornflakes, crushed
- ¼ cup shredded coconut
- 8 slices oat nut bread or any whole-grain, oversize bread
- 6 tablespoons peanut butter
- 2 medium bananas, cut into ½-inch-thick slices
- 6 tablespoons pineapple preserves
- 1 egg, beaten
- oil for misting or cooking spray

Directions:

1. Preheat air fryer to 360°F.
2. In a shallow dish, mix together the cornflake crumbs and coconut.
3. For each sandwich, spread one bread slice with 1½ tablespoons of peanut butter. Top with banana slices. Spread another bread slice with 1½ tablespoons of preserves. Combine to make a sandwich.
4. Using a pastry brush, brush top of sandwich lightly with beaten egg. Sprinkle with about 1½ tablespoons of crumb coating, pressing it in to make it stick. Spray with oil.
5. Turn sandwich over and repeat to coat and spray the other side.
6. Cooking 2 at a time, place sandwiches in air fryer basket and cook for 6 to 7minutes or until coating is golden brown and crispy. If sandwich doesn't brown enough, spray with a little more oil and cook at 390°F for another minute.
7. Cut cooked sandwiches in half and serve warm.

Hush Puffins

Servings: 20

Cooking Time: 8 Minutes

Ingredients:

- 1 cup buttermilk
- ¼ cup butter, melted
- 2 eggs
- 1½ cups all-purpose flour
- 1½ cups cornmeal
- ⅓ cup sugar
- 1 teaspoon baking soda
- 1 teaspoon salt
- 4 scallions, minced
- vegetable oil

Directions:

1. Combine the buttermilk, butter and eggs in a large mixing bowl. In a second bowl combine the flour, cornmeal, sugar, baking soda and salt. Add the dry ingredients to the wet ingredients, stirring just to combine. Stir in the minced scallions and refrigerate the batter for 30 minutes.
2. Shape the batter into 2-inch balls. Brush or spray the balls with oil.
3. Preheat the air fryer to 360°F.
4. Air-fry the hush puffins in two batches at 360°F for 8 minutes, turning them over after 6 minutes of the cooking process.
5. Serve warm with butter.

Bacon Puff Pastry Pinwheels

Servings: 8

Cooking Time: 10 Minutes

Ingredients:

➢ 1 sheet of puff pastry

➢ 2 tablespoons maple syrup

➢ ¼ cup brown sugar

➢ 8 slices bacon (not thick cut)

➢ coarsely cracked black pepper

➢ vegetable oil

Directions:

1. On a lightly floured surface, roll the puff pastry out into a square that measures roughly 10 inches wide by however long your bacon strips are (usually about 11 inches). Cut the pastry into eight even strips.

2. Brush the strips of pastry with the maple syrup and sprinkle the brown sugar on top, leaving 1 inch of dough exposed at the far end of each strip. Place a slice of bacon on each strip of puff pastry, letting 1/8-inch of the length of bacon hang over the edge of the pastry. Season generously with coarsely ground black pepper.

3. With the exposed end of the pastry strips away from you, roll the bacon and pastry strips up into pinwheels. Dab a little water on the exposed end of the pastry and pinch it to the pinwheel to seal the pastry shut.

4. Preheat the air fryer to 360°F.

5. Brush or spray the air fryer basket with a little vegetable oil. Place the pinwheels into the basket and air-fry at 360°F for 8 minutes. Turn the pinwheels over and air-fry for another 2 minutes to brown the bottom. Serve warm.

VEGETABLE SIDE DISHES RECIPES

Street Corn

Servings: 4

Cooking Time: 10 Minutes

Ingredients:

➢ 1 tablespoon butter

➢ 4 ears corn

➢ ⅓ cup plain Greek yogurt

➢ 2 tablespoons Parmesan cheese

➢ ½ teaspoon paprika

➢ ½ teaspoon garlic powder

➢ ¼ teaspoon salt

➢ ¼ teaspoon black pepper

➢ ¼ cup finely chopped cilantro

Directions:

1. Preheat the air fryer to 400°F.

2. In a medium microwave-safe bowl, melt the butter in the microwave. Lightly brush the outside of the ears of corn with the melted butter.

3. Place the corn into the air fryer basket and cook for 5 minutes, flip the corn, and cook another 5 minutes.

4. Meanwhile, in a medium bowl, mix the yogurt, cheese, paprika, garlic powder, salt, and pepper. Set aside.

5. Carefully remove the corn from the air fryer and let cool 3 minutes. Brush the outside edges with the yogurt mixture and top with fresh chopped cilantro. Serve immediately.

Roasted Corn Salad

Servings: 3

Cooking Time: 15 Minutes

Ingredients:

- 3 4-inch lengths husked and de-silked corn on the cob
- Olive oil spray
- 1 cup Packed baby arugula leaves
- 12 Cherry tomatoes, halved
- Up to 3 Medium scallion(s), trimmed and thinly sliced
- 2 tablespoons Lemon juice
- 1 tablespoon Olive oil
- 1½ teaspoons Honey
- ¼ teaspoon Mild paprika
- ¼ teaspoon Dried oregano
- ¼ teaspoon, plus more to taste Table salt
- ¼ teaspoon Ground black pepper

Directions:

1. Preheat the air fryer to 400°F.

2. When the machine is at temperature, lightly coat the pieces of corn on the cob with olive oil spray. Set the pieces of corn in the basket with as much air space between them as possible. Air-fry undisturbed for 15 minutes, or until the corn is charred in a few spots.

3. Use kitchen tongs to transfer the corn to a wire rack. Cool for 15 minutes.

4. Cut the kernels off the ears by cutting the fat end off each piece so it will stand up straight on a cutting board, then running a knife down the corn. (Or you can save your fingers and buy a fancy tool to remove kernels from corn cobs. Check it out at online kitchenware stores.) Scoop the kernels into a serving bowl.

5. Chop the arugula into bite-size bits and add these to the kernels. Add the tomatoes and scallions, too. Whisk the lemon juice, olive oil, honey, paprika, oregano, salt, and pepper in a small bowl until the honey dissolves. Pour over the salad and toss well to coat, tasting for extra salt before serving.

Creole Potato Wedges

Servings: 4

Cooking Time: 10 Minutes

Ingredients:

➢ 1 pound medium Yukon gold potatoes
➢ ½ teaspoon cayenne pepper
➢ ½ teaspoon thyme
➢ ½ teaspoon garlic powder
➢ ½ teaspoon salt
➢ ½ teaspoon smoked paprika
➢ 1 cup dry breadcrumbs
➢ oil for misting or cooking spray

Directions:

1. Wash potatoes, cut into thick wedges, and drop wedges into a bowl of water to prevent browning.

2. Mix together the cayenne pepper, thyme, garlic powder, salt, paprika, and breadcrumbs and spread on a sheet of wax paper.

3. Remove potatoes from water and, without drying them, roll in the breadcrumb mixture.

4. Spray air fryer basket with oil or cooking spray and pile potato wedges into basket. It's okay if they form more than a single layer.

5. Cook at 390°F for 8minutes. Shake basket, then continue cooking for 2 minutes longer, until coating is crisp and potato centers are soft. Total cooking time will vary, depending on thickness of potato wedges.

Okra

Servings: 4

Cooking Time: 12 Minutes

Ingredients:

- ➢ 7–8 ounces fresh okra
- ➢ 1 egg
- ➢ 1 cup milk
- ➢ 1 cup breadcrumbs
- ➢ ½ teaspoon salt
- ➢ oil for misting or cooking spray

Directions:

1. Remove stem ends from okra and cut in ½-inch slices.
2. In a medium bowl, beat together egg and milk. Add okra slices and stir to coat.
3. In a sealable plastic bag or container with lid, mix together the breadcrumbs and salt.
4. Remove okra from egg mixture, letting excess drip off, and transfer into bag with breadcrumbs.
5. Shake okra in crumbs to coat well.
6. Place all of the coated okra into the air fryer basket and mist with oil or cooking spray. Okra doesn't need to cook in a single layer, nor is it necessary to spray all sides at this point. A good spritz on top will do.
7. Cook at 390°F for 5minutes. Shake basket to redistribute and give it another spritz as you shake.
8. Cook 5 more minutes. Shake and spray again. Cook for 2 minutes longer or until golden brown and crispy.

Chicken Eggrolls

Servings: 10

Cooking Time: 17 Minutes

Ingredients:

- ➢ 1 tablespoon vegetable oil
- ➢ ¼ cup chopped onion
- ➢ 1 clove garlic, minced
- ➢ 1 cup shredded carrot
- ➢ ½ cup thinly sliced celery
- ➢ 2 cups cooked chicken
- ➢ 2 cups shredded white cabbage
- ➢ ½ cup teriyaki sauce
- ➢ 20 egg roll wrappers
- ➢ 1 egg, whisked
- ➢ 1 tablespoon water

Directions:

1. Preheat the air fryer to 390°F.

2. In a large skillet, heat the oil over medium-high heat. Add in the onion and sauté for 1 minute. Add in the garlic and sauté for 30 seconds. Add in the carrot and celery and cook for 2 minutes. Add in the chicken, cabbage, and teriyaki sauce. Allow the mixture to cook for 1 minute, stirring to combine. Remove from the heat.

3. In a small bowl, whisk together the egg and water for brushing the edges.

4. Lay the eggroll wrappers out at an angle. Place ¼ cup filling in the center. Fold the bottom corner up first and then fold in the corners; roll up to complete eggroll.

5. Place the eggrolls in the air fryer basket, spray with cooking spray, and cook for 8 minutes, turn over, and cook another 2 to 4 minutes.

Curried Cauliflower With Cashews And Yogurt

Servings: 2

Cooking Time: 12 Minutes

Ingredients:

- ➤ 4 cups cauliflower florets (about half a large head)
- ➤ 1 tablespoon olive oil
- ➤ salt
- ➤ 1 teaspoon curry powder
- ➤ ½ cup toasted, chopped cashews
- ➤ Cool Yogurt Drizzle
- ➤ ¼ cup plain yogurt
- ➤ 2 tablespoons sour cream
- ➤ 1 teaspoon lemon juice
- ➤ pinch cayenne pepper
- ➤ salt
- ➤ 1 teaspoon honey
- ➤ 1 tablespoon chopped fresh cilantro, plus leaves for garnish

Directions:

1. Preheat the air fryer to 400°F.

2. Toss the cauliflower florets with the olive oil, salt and curry powder, coating evenly.

3. Transfer the cauliflower to the air fryer basket and air-fry at 400°F for 12 minutes, shaking the basket a couple of times during the cooking process.

4. While the cauliflower is cooking, make the cool yogurt drizzle by combining all ingredients in a bowl.

5. When the cauliflower is cooked to your liking, serve it warm with the cool yogurt either underneath or drizzled over the top. Scatter the cashews and cilantro leaves around.

Blistered Tomatoes

Servings: 20

Cooking Time: 15 Minutes

Ingredients:

➤ 1½ pounds Cherry or grape tomatoes

➤ Olive oil spray

➤ 1½ teaspoons Balsamic vinegar

➤ ¼ teaspoon Table salt

➤ ¼ teaspoon Ground black pepper

Directions:

1. Put the basket in a drawer-style air fryer, or a baking tray in the lower third of a toaster oven–style air fryer. Place a 6-inch round cake pan in the basket or on the tray for a small batch, a 7-inch round cake pan for a medium batch, or an 8-inch round cake pan for a large one. Heat the air fryer to 400°F with the pan in the basket. When the machine is at temperature, keep heating the pan for 5 minutes more.

2. Place the tomatoes in a large bowl, coat them with the olive oil spray, toss gently, then spritz a couple of times more, tossing after each spritz, until the tomatoes are glistening.

3. Pour the tomatoes into the cake pan and air-fry undisturbed for 10 minutes, or until they split and begin to brown.

4. Use kitchen tongs and a nonstick-safe spatula, or silicone baking mitts, to remove the cake pan from the basket. Toss the hot tomatoes with the vinegar, salt, and pepper. Cool in the pan for a few minutes before serving.

French Fries

Servings: 4

Cooking Time: 25 Minutes

Ingredients:

➢ 2 cups fresh potatoes

➢ 2 teaspoons oil

➢ ½ teaspoon salt

Directions:

1. Cut potatoes into ½-inch-wide slices, then lay slices flat and cut into ½-inch sticks.

2. Rinse potato sticks and blot dry with a clean towel.

3. In a bowl or sealable plastic bag, mix the potatoes, oil, and salt together.

4. Pour into air fryer basket.

5. Cook at 390°F for 10minutes. Shake basket to redistribute fries and continue cooking for approximately 15minutes, until fries are golden brown.

Onions

Servings: 4

Cooking Time: 18 Minutes

Ingredients:

➤ 2 yellow onions (Vidalia or 1015 recommended)

➤ salt and pepper

➤ ¼ teaspoon ground thyme

➤ ¼ teaspoon smoked paprika

➤ 2 teaspoons olive oil

➤ 1 ounce Gruyère cheese, grated

Directions:

1. Peel onions and halve lengthwise (vertically).

2. Sprinkle cut sides of onions with salt, pepper, thyme, and paprika.

3. Place each onion half, cut-surface up, on a large square of aluminum foil. Pull sides of foil up to cup around onion. Drizzle cut surface of onions with oil.

4. Crimp foil at top to seal closed.

5. Place wrapped onions in air fryer basket and cook at 390°F for 18 minutes. When done, onions should be soft enough to pierce with fork but still slightly firm.

6. Open foil just enough to sprinkle each onion with grated cheese.

7. Cook for 30 seconds to 1 minute to melt cheese.

Beet Fries

Servings: 3

Cooking Time: 22 Minutes

Ingredients:

- ➢ 3 6-ounce red beets
- ➢ Vegetable oil spray
- ➢ To taste Coarse sea salt or kosher salt

Directions:

1. Preheat the air fryer to 375°F .
2. Remove the stems from the beets and peel them with a knife or vegetable peeler. Slice them into ½-inch-thick circles. Lay these flat on a cutting board and slice them into ½-inch-thick sticks. Generously coat the sticks on all sides with vegetable oil spray.
3. When the machine is at temperature, drop them into the basket, shake the basket to even the sticks out into as close to one layer as possible, and air-fry for 20 minutes, tossing and rearranging the beet matchsticks every 5 minutes, or until brown and even crisp at the ends. If the machine is at 360°F, you may need to add 2 minutes to the cooking time.
4. Pour the fries into a big bowl, add the salt, toss well, and serve warm.

Tandoori Cauliflower

Servings: 4

Cooking Time: 10 Minutes

Ingredients:

➤ ½ cup Plain full-fat yogurt (not Greek yogurt)

➤ 1½ teaspoons Yellow curry powder, purchased or homemade (see the headnote)

➤ 1½ teaspoons Lemon juice

➤ ¾ teaspoon Table salt (optional)

➤ 4½ cups (about 1 pound 2 ounces) 2-inch cauliflower florets

Directions:

1. Preheat the air fryer to 400°F.

2. Whisk the yogurt, curry powder, lemon juice, and salt (if using) in a large bowl until uniform. Add the florets and stir gently to coat the florets well and evenly. Even better, use your clean, dry hands to get the yogurt mixture down into all the nooks of the florets.

3. When the machine is at temperature, transfer the florets to the basket, spreading them gently into as close to one layer as you can. Air-fry for 10 minutes, tossing and rearranging the florets twice so that any covered or touching parts are exposed to the air currents, until lightly browned and tender if still a bit crunchy.

4. Pour the contents of the basket onto a wire rack. Cool for at least 5 minutes before serving, or serve at room temperature.

Buttermilk Biscuits

Servings: 5	Cooking Time: 14 Minutes

Ingredients:

- 1⅔ cups, plus more for dusting All-purpose flour
- 1½ teaspoons Baking powder
- ¼ teaspoon Table salt

- 3 tablespoons plus 1 teaspoon Butter, cold and cut into small pieces
- ½ cup plus ½ tablespoon Cold buttermilk, regular or low-fat
- 2½ tablespoons Butter, melted and cooled

Directions:

1. Preheat the air fryer to 400°F.

2. Mix the flour, baking powder, and salt in a large bowl. Use a pastry cutter or a sturdy flatware fork to cut the cold butter pieces into the flour mixture, working the fat through the tines again and again until the mixture resembles coarse dry sand. Stir in the buttermilk to make a dough.

3. Very lightly dust a clean, dry work surface with flour. Turn the dough out onto it, dip your clean hands into flour, and press the dough into a ¾-inch-thick circle. Use a 3-inch round cookie cutter or sturdy drinking glass to cut the dough into rounds. Gather the dough scraps together, lightly shape again into a ¾-inch-thick circle, and cut out a few more rounds. You'll end up with 4 raw biscuits for a small air fryer, 5 for a medium, or 6 for a large.

4. For a small air fryer, brush the inside of a 6-inch round cake pan with a little more than half of the melted butter, then set the 4 raw biscuits in it, letting them touch but without squishing them.

5. For a medium air fryer, do the same with half of the melted butter in a 7-inch round cake pan and 5 raw biscuits.

6. And for a large air fryer, use a little more than half the melted butter to brush the inside of an 8-inch round cake pan, and set the 6 raw biscuits in it in the same way.

7. Brush the tops of the raw biscuits with the remaining melted butter.

8. Air-fry undisturbed for 14 minutes, or until the biscuits are golden brown and dry to the touch.

9. Using kitchen tongs and a nonstick-safe spatula, two hot pads, or silicone baking mitts, remove the cake pan from the basket and set it on a wire rack. Cool undisturbed for a couple of minutes. Turn the biscuits out onto the wire rack to cool for a couple of minutes more before serving.

BEEF , PORK & LAMB RECIPES

Pepper Steak

Servings: 4

Cooking Time: 30 Minutes

Ingredients:

➢ 2 tablespoons cornstarch

➢ 1 tablespoon sugar

➢ ¾ cup beef broth

➢ ¼ cup hoisin sauce

➢ 3 tablespoons soy sauce

➢ 1 teaspoon sesame oil

➢ ½ teaspoon freshly ground black pepper

➢ 1½ pounds boneless New York strip steaks, sliced into ½-inch strips

➢ 1 onion, sliced

➢ 3 small bell peppers, red, yellow and green, sliced

Directions:

1. Whisk the cornstarch and sugar together in a large bowl to break up any lumps in the cornstarch. Add the beef broth and whisk until combined and smooth. Stir in the hoisin sauce, soy sauce, sesame oil and freshly ground black pepper. Add the beef, onion and peppers, and toss to coat. Marinate the beef and vegetables at room temperature for 30 minutes, stirring a few times to keep meat and vegetables coated.

2. Preheat the air fryer to 350°F.

3. Transfer the beef, onion, and peppers to the air fryer basket with tongs, reserving the marinade. Air-fry the beef and vegetables for 30 minutes, stirring well two or three times during the cooking process.

4. While the beef is air-frying, bring the reserved marinade to a simmer in a small saucepan over medium heat on the stovetop. Simmer for 5 minutes until the sauce thickens.

5. When the steak and vegetables have finished cooking, transfer them to a serving platter. Pour the hot sauce over the pepper steak and serve with white rice.

Sausage-cheese Calzone

Servings: 8	Cooking Time: 8 Minutes

Ingredients:

- ➤ Crust
- ➤ 2 cups white wheat flour, plus more for kneading and rolling
- ➤ 1 package (¼ ounce) RapidRise yeast
- ➤ 1 teaspoon salt
- ➤ ½ teaspoon dried basil
- ➤ 1 cup warm water (115°F to 125°F)
- ➤ 2 teaspoons olive oil

- ➤ Filling
- ➤ ¼ pound Italian sausage
- ➤ ½ cup ricotta cheese
- ➤ 4 ounces mozzarella cheese, shredded
- ➤ ¼ cup grated Parmesan cheese
- ➤ oil for misting or cooking spray
- ➤ marinara sauce for serving

Directions:

1. Crumble Italian sausage into air fryer baking pan and cook at 390°F for 5minutes. Stir, breaking apart, and cook for 3 to 4minutes, until well done. Remove and set aside on paper towels to drain.

2. To make dough, combine flour, yeast, salt, and basil. Add warm water and oil and stir until a soft dough forms. Turn out onto lightly floured board and knead for 3 or 4minutes. Let dough rest for 10minutes.

3. To make filling, combine the three cheeses in a medium bowl and mix well. Stir in the cooked sausage.

4. Cut dough into 8 pieces.

5. Working with 4 pieces of the dough, press each into a circle about 5 inches in diameter. Top each dough circle with 2 heaping tablespoons of filling. Fold over to create a half-moon shape and press edges firmly together. Be sure that edges are firmly sealed to prevent leakage. Spray both sides with oil or cooking spray.

6. Place 4 calzones in air fryer basket and cook at 360°F for 5minutes. Mist with oil and cook for 3 minutes, until crust is done and nicely browned.

7. While the first batch is cooking, press out the remaining dough, fill, and shape into calzones.

8. Spray both sides with oil and cook for 5minutes. If needed, mist with oil and continue cooking for 3 minutes longer. This second batch will cook a little faster than the first because your air fryer is already hot.

9. Serve with marinara sauce on the side for dipping.

Lollipop Lamb Chops With Mint Pesto

Servings: 4

Cooking Time: 7 Minutes

Ingredients:

➤ Mint Pesto

➤ ½ small clove garlic

➤ ¼ cup packed fresh parsley

➤ ¾ cup packed fresh mint

➤ ½ teaspoon lemon juice

➤ ¼ cup grated Parmesan cheese

➤ ⅓ cup shelled pistachios

➤ ¼ teaspoon salt

➤ ½ cup olive oil

➤ 8 "frenched" lamb chops (1 rack)

➤ olive oil

➤ salt and freshly ground black pepper

➤ 1 tablespoon dried rosemary, chopped

➤ 1 tablespoon dried thyme

Directions:

1. Make the pesto by combining the garlic, parsley and mint in a food processor and process until finely chopped. Add the lemon juice, Parmesan cheese, pistachios and salt. Process until all the ingredients have turned into a paste. With the processor running, slowly pour the olive oil in through the feed tube. Scrape the sides of the processor with a spatula and process for another 30 seconds.

2. Preheat the air fryer to 400°F.

3. Rub both sides of the lamb chops with olive oil and season with salt, pepper, rosemary and thyme, pressing the herbs into the meat gently with your fingers. Transfer the lamb chops to the air fryer basket.

4. Air-fry the lamb chops at 400°F for 5 minutes. Flip the chops over and air-fry for an additional 2 minutes. This should bring the chops to a medium-rare doneness, depending on their thickness. Adjust the cooking time up or down a minute or two accordingly for different degrees of doneness.

5. Serve the lamb chops with mint pesto drizzled on top.

Chicken-fried Steak

Servings: 2

Cooking Time: 12 Minutes

Ingredients:

➤ 1½ cups All-purpose flour

➤ 2 Large egg(s)

➤ 2 tablespoons Regular or low-fat sour cream

➤ 2 tablespoons Worcestershire sauce

➤ 2 ¼-pound thin beef cube steak(s)

➤ Vegetable oil spray

Directions:

1. Preheat the air fryer to 400°F.

2. Set up and fill two shallow soup plates or small pie plates on your counter: one for the flour; and one for the egg(s), whisked with the sour cream and Worcestershire sauce until uniform.

3. Dredge a piece of beef in the flour, coating it well on both sides and even along the edge. Shake off any excess; then dip the meat in the egg mixture, coating both sides while retaining the flour on the meat. Let any excess egg mixture slip back into the rest. Dredge the meat in the flour once again, coating all surfaces well. Gently shake off the excess coating and set the steak aside if you're coating another steak or two. Once done, coat the steak(s) on both sides with the vegetable oil spray.

4. Set the steak(s) in the basket. If there's more than one steak, make sure they do not overlap or even touch, although the smallest gap between them is enough to get them crunchy. Air-fry undisturbed for 6 minutes.

5. Use kitchen tongs to pick up one of the steaks. Coat it again on both sides with vegetable oil spray. Turn it upside down and set it back in the basket with that same regard for the space between them in larger batches. Repeat with any other steaks. Continue air-frying undisturbed for 6 minutes, or until golden brown and crunchy.

6. Use kitchen tongs to transfer the steak(s) to a wire rack. Cool for 5 minutes before serving.

Calf's Liver

Servings: 4

Cooking Time: 5 Minutes

Ingredients:

➢ 1 pound sliced calf's liver
➢ salt and pepper
➢ 2 eggs
➢ 2 tablespoons milk
➢ ½ cup whole wheat flour
➢ 1½ cups panko breadcrumbs
➢ ½ cup plain breadcrumbs
➢ ½ teaspoon salt
➢ ¼ teaspoon pepper
➢ oil for misting or cooking spray

Directions:

1. Cut liver slices crosswise into strips about ½-inch wide. Sprinkle with salt and pepper to taste.

2. Beat together egg and milk in a shallow dish.

3. Place wheat flour in a second shallow dish.

4. In a third shallow dish, mix together panko, plain breadcrumbs, ½ teaspoon salt, and ¼ teaspoon pepper.

5. Preheat air fryer to 390°F.

6. Dip liver strips in flour, egg wash, and then breadcrumbs, pressing in coating slightly to make crumbs stick.

7. Cooking half the liver at a time, place strips in air fryer basket in a single layer, close but not touching. Cook at 390°F for 5 minutes or until done to your preference.

8. Repeat step 7 to cook remaining liver.

Skirt Steak Fajitas

Servings: 4	Cooking Time: 30 Minutes

Ingredients:

- 2 tablespoons olive oil
- ¼ cup lime juice
- 1 clove garlic, minced
- ½ teaspoon ground cumin
- ½ teaspoon hot sauce
- ½ teaspoon salt
- 2 tablespoons chopped fresh cilantro
- 1 pound skirt steak
- 1 onion, sliced

- 1 teaspoon chili powder
- 1 red pepper, sliced
- 1 green pepper, sliced
- salt and freshly ground black pepper
- 8 flour tortillas
- shredded lettuce, crumbled Queso Fresco (or grated Cheddar cheese), sliced black olives, diced tomatoes, sour cream and guacamole for serving

Directions:

1. Combine the olive oil, lime juice, garlic, cumin, hot sauce, salt and cilantro in a shallow dish. Add the skirt steak and turn it over several times to coat all sides. Pierce the steak with a needle-style meat tenderizer or paring knife. Marinate the steak in the refrigerator for at least 3 hours, or overnight. When you are ready to cook, remove the steak from the refrigerator and let it sit at room temperature for 30 minutes.

2. Preheat the air fryer to 400°F.

3. Toss the onion slices with the chili powder and a little olive oil and transfer them to the air fryer basket. Air-fry at 400°F for 5 minutes. Add the red and green peppers to the air fryer basket with the onions, season with salt and pepper and air-fry for 8 more minutes, until the onions and peppers are soft. Transfer the vegetables to a dish and cover with aluminum foil to keep warm.

4. Place the skirt steak in the air fryer basket and pour the marinade over the top. Air-fry at 400°F for 12 minutes. Flip the steak over and air-fry at 400°F for an additional 5 minutes. (The time needed for your steak will depend on the thickness of the skirt steak. 17 minutes should bring your steak to roughly medium.) Transfer the cooked steak to a cutting board and let the steak rest for a few minutes. If the peppers and onions need to be heated, return them to the air fryer for just 1 to 2 minutes.

5. Thinly slice the steak at an angle, cutting against the grain of the steak. Serve the steak with the onions and peppers, the warm tortillas and the fajita toppings on the side so that everyone can make their own fajita.

Kielbasa Chunks With Pineapple & Peppers

Servings: 2

Cooking Time: 10 Minutes

Ingredients:

- ¾ pound kielbasa sausage
- 1 cup bell pepper chunks (any color)
- 1 8-ounce can pineapple chunks in juice, drained
- 1 tablespoon barbeque seasoning
- 1 tablespoon soy sauce
- cooking spray

Directions:

1. Cut sausage into ½-inch slices.
2. In a medium bowl, toss all ingredients together.
3. Spray air fryer basket with nonstick cooking spray.
4. Pour sausage mixture into the basket.
5. Cook at 390°F for approximately 5minutes. Shake basket and cook an additional 5minutes.

Vietnamese Shaking Beef

Servings: 3

Cooking Time: 7 Minutes

Ingredients:

- ➤ 1 pound Beef tenderloin, cut into 1-inch cubes
- ➤ 1 tablespoon Regular or low-sodium soy sauce or gluten-free tamari sauce
- ➤ 1 tablespoon Fish sauce (gluten-free, if a concern)
- ➤ 1 tablespoon Dark brown sugar
- ➤ 1½ teaspoons Ground black pepper
- ➤ 3 Medium scallions, trimmed and thinly sliced
- ➤ 2 tablespoons Butter
- ➤ 1½ teaspoons Minced garlic

Directions:

1. Mix the beef, soy or tamari sauce, fish sauce, and brown sugar in a bowl until well combined. Cover and refrigerate for at least 2 hours or up to 8 hours, tossing the beef at least twice in the marinade.

2. Put a 6-inch round or square cake pan in an air-fryer basket for a small batch, a 7-inch round or square cake pan for a medium batch, or an 8-inch round or square cake pan for a large one. Or put one of these on the rack of a toaster oven–style air fryer. Heat the machine with the pan in it to 400°F. When the machine it at temperature, let the pan sit in the heat for 2 to 3 minutes so that it gets very hot.

3. Use a slotted spoon to transfer the beef to the pan, leaving any marinade behind in the bowl. Spread the meat into as close to an even layer as you can. Air-fry undisturbed for 5 minutes. Meanwhile, discard the marinade, if any.

4. Add the scallions, butter, and garlic to the beef. Air-fry for 2 minutes, tossing and rearranging the beef and scallions repeatedly, perhaps every 20 seconds.

5. Remove the basket from the machine and let the meat cool in the pan for a couple of minutes before serving.

Beef And Spinach Braciole

Servings: 4   Cooking Time: 92 Minutes

Ingredients:

- 7-inch oven-safe baking pan or casserole
- ½ onion, finely chopped
- 1 teaspoon olive oil
- ⅓ cup red wine
- 2 cups crushed tomatoes
- 1 teaspoon Italian seasoning
- ½ teaspoon garlic powder
- ¼ teaspoon crushed red pepper flakes
- 2 tablespoons chopped fresh parsley

- 2 top round steaks (about 1½ pounds)
- salt and freshly ground black pepper
- 2 cups fresh spinach, chopped
- 1 clove minced garlic
- ½ cup roasted red peppers, julienned
- ½ cup grated pecorino cheese
- ¼ cup pine nuts, toasted and rough chopped
- 2 tablespoons olive oil

Directions:

1. Preheat the air fryer to 400°F.

2. Toss the onions and olive oil together in a 7-inch metal baking pan or casserole dish. Air-fry at 400°F for 5 minutes, stirring a couple times during the cooking process. Add the red wine, crushed tomatoes, Italian seasoning, garlic powder, red pepper flakes and parsley and stir. Cover the pan tightly with aluminum foil, lower the air fryer temperature to 350°F and continue to air-fry for 15 minutes.

3. While the sauce is simmering, prepare the beef. Using a meat mallet, pound the beef until it is ¼-inch thick. Season both sides of the beef with salt and pepper. Combine the spinach, garlic, red peppers, pecorino cheese, pine nuts and olive oil in a medium bowl. Season with salt and freshly ground black pepper. Spread the mixture evenly over the steaks. Starting at one of the short ends, roll the beef around the filling, tucking in the sides as you roll to ensure the filling is completely enclosed. Secure the beef rolls with toothpicks.

4. Remove the baking pan with the sauce from the air fryer and set it aside. Preheat the air fryer to 400°F.

5. Brush or spray the beef rolls with a little olive oil and air-fry at 400°F for 12 minutes, rotating the beef during the cooking process for even browning. When the beef is browned, submerge the rolls into the sauce in the baking pan, cover the pan with foil and return it to the air fryer. Air-fry at 250°F for 60 minutes.

6. Remove the beef rolls from the sauce. Cut each roll into slices and serve with pasta, ladling some of the sauce overtop.

Pork Cutlets With Almond-lemon Crust

Servings: 3

Cooking Time: 14 Minutes

Ingredients:

➢ ¾ cup Almond flour

➢ ¾ cup Plain dried bread crumbs (gluten-free, if a concern)

➢ 1½ teaspoons Finely grated lemon zest

➢ 1¼ teaspoons Table salt

➢ ¾ teaspoon Garlic powder

➢ ¾ teaspoon Dried oregano

➢ 1 Large egg white(s)

➢ 2 tablespoons Water

➢ 3 6-ounce center-cut boneless pork loin chops (about ¾ inch thick)

➢ Olive oil spray

Directions:

1. Preheat the air fryer to 375°F .

2. Mix the almond flour, bread crumbs, lemon zest, salt, garlic powder, and dried oregano in a large bowl until well combined.

3. Whisk the egg white(s) and water in a shallow soup plate or small pie plate until uniform.

4. Dip a chop in the egg white mixture, turning it to coat all sides, even the ends. Let any excess egg white mixture slip back into the rest, then set it in the almond flour mixture. Turn it several times, pressing gently to coat it evenly. Generously coat the chop with olive oil spray, then set aside to dip and coat the remaining chop(s).

5. Set the chops in the basket with as much air space between them as possible. Air-fry undisturbed for 12 minutes, or until browned and crunchy. You may need to add 2 minutes to the cooking time if the machine is at 360°F.

6. Use kitchen tongs to transfer the chops to a wire rack. Cool for a few minutes before serving.

Italian Sausage & Peppers

Servings: 6

Cooking Time: 25 Minutes

Ingredients:

- 1 6-ounce can tomato paste
- ⅔ cup water
- 1 8-ounce can tomato sauce
- 1 teaspoon dried parsley flakes
- ½ teaspoon garlic powder
- ⅛ teaspoon oregano
- ½ pound mild Italian bulk sausage
- 1 tablespoon extra virgin olive oil
- ½ large onion, cut in 1-inch chunks
- 4 ounces fresh mushrooms, sliced
- 1 large green bell pepper, cut in 1-inch chunks
- 8 ounces spaghetti, cooked
- Parmesan cheese for serving

Directions:

1. In a large saucepan or skillet, stir together the tomato paste, water, tomato sauce, parsley, garlic, and oregano. Heat on stovetop over very low heat while preparing meat and vegetables.

2. Break sausage into small chunks, about ½-inch pieces. Place in air fryer baking pan.

3. Cook at 390°F for 5minutes. Stir. Cook 7 minutes longer or until sausage is well done. Remove from pan, drain on paper towels, and add to the sauce mixture.

4. If any sausage grease remains in baking pan, pour it off or use paper towels to soak it up. (Be careful handling that hot pan!)

5. Place olive oil, onions, and mushrooms in pan and stir. Cook for 5minutes or just until tender. Using a slotted spoon, transfer onions and mushrooms from baking pan into the sauce and sausage mixture.

6. Place bell pepper chunks in air fryer baking pan and cook for 8 minutes or until tender. When done, stir into sauce with sausage and other vegetables.

7. Serve over cooked spaghetti with plenty of Parmesan cheese.

Albóndigas

Servings: 4

Cooking Time: 15 Minutes

Ingredients:

➢ 1 pound Lean ground pork

➢ 3 tablespoons Very finely chopped trimmed scallions

➢ 3 tablespoons Finely chopped fresh cilantro leaves

➢ 3 tablespoons Plain panko bread crumbs (gluten-free, if a concern)

➢ 3 tablespoons Dry white wine, dry sherry, or unsweetened apple juice

➢ 1½ teaspoons Minced garlic

➢ 1¼ teaspoons Mild smoked paprika

➢ ¾ teaspoon Dried oregano

➢ ¾ teaspoon Table salt

➢ ¼ teaspoon Ground black pepper

➢ Olive oil spray

Directions:

1. Preheat the air fryer to 400°F.

2. Mix the ground pork, scallions, cilantro, bread crumbs, wine or its substitute, garlic, smoked paprika, oregano, salt, and pepper in a bowl until the herbs and spices are evenly distributed in the mixture.

3. Lightly coat your clean hands with olive oil spray, then form the ground pork mixture into balls, using 2 tablespoons for each one. Spray your hands frequently so that the meat mixture doesn't stick.

4. Set the balls in the basket so that they're not touching, even if they're close together. Air-fry undisturbed for 15 minutes, or until well browned and an instant-read meat thermometer inserted into one or two balls registers 165°F.

5. Use a nonstick-safe spatula and kitchen tongs for balance to gently transfer the fragile balls to a wire rack to cool for 5 minutes before serving.

APPETIZERS AND SNACKS

Crab Rangoon

Servings: 18   Cooking Time: 6 Minutes

Ingredients:

- 4½ tablespoons (a little more than ¼ pound) Crabmeat, preferably backfin or claw, picked over for shells and cartilage
- 1½ ounces (3 tablespoons) Regular or low-fat cream cheese (not fat-free), softened to room temperature

- 1½ tablespoons Minced scallion
- 1½ teaspoons Minced garlic
- 1½ teaspoons Worcestershire sauce
- 18 Wonton wrappers (thawed, if necessary)
- Vegetable oil spray

Directions:

1. Preheat the air fryer to 400°F.

2. Gently stir the crab, cream cheese, scallion, garlic, and Worcestershire sauce in a medium bowl until well combined.

3. Set a bowl of water on a clean, dry work surface or next to a large cutting board. Set one wonton wrapper on the surface, then put a teaspoonful of the crab mixture in the center of the wrapper. Dip your clean finger in the water and run it around the edge of the wrapper. Bring all four sides up to the center and over the filling, and pinch them together in the middle to seal without covering all of the filling. The traditional look is for the corners of the filled wonton to become four open "flower petals" radiating out from the filled center. Set the filled wonton aside and continue making more as needed. (If you want a video tutorial on filling these, see ours at our YouTube channel, Cooking with Bruce and Mark.)

4. Generously coat the filled wontons with vegetable oil spray. Set them sealed side up in the basket with a little room among them. Air-fry undisturbed for 6 minutes, or until golden brown and crisp.

5. Use a nonstick-safe spatula to gently transfer the wontons to a wire rack. Cool for 5 minutes before serving warm.

Veggie Chips

Servings: X

Cooking Time: X

Ingredients:

➢ sweet potato

➢ large parsnip

➢ large carrot

➢ turnip

➢ large beet

➢ vegetable or canola oil, in a spray bottle

➢ salt

Directions:

1. You can do a medley of vegetable chips, or just select from the vegetables listed. Whatever you choose to do, scrub the vegetables well and then slice them paper-thin using a mandolin (about -1/16 inch thick).

2. Preheat the air fryer to 400°F.

3. Air-fry the chips in batches, one type of vegetable at a time. Spray the chips lightly with oil and transfer them to the air fryer basket. The key is to NOT over-load the basket. You can overlap the chips a little, but don't pile them on top of each other. Doing so will make it much harder to get evenly browned and crispy chips. Air-fry at 400°F for the time indicated below, shaking the basket several times during the cooking process for even cooking.

4. Sweet Potato – 8 to 9 minutes

5. Parsnips – 5 minutes

6. Carrot – 7 minutes

7. Turnips – 8 minutes

8. Beets – 9 minutes

9. Season the chips with salt during the last couple of minutes of air-frying. Check the chips as they cook until they are done to your liking. Some will start to brown sooner than others.

10. You can enjoy the chips warm out of the air fryer or cool them to room temperature for crispier chips.

Fried Pickles

Servings: 2

Cooking Time: 15 Minutes

Ingredients:

- 1 egg
- 1 tablespoon milk
- ¼ teaspoon hot sauce
- 2 cups sliced dill pickles, well drained
- ¾ cup breadcrumbs
- oil for misting or cooking spray

Directions:

1. Preheat air fryer to 390°F.
2. Beat together egg, milk, and hot sauce in a bowl large enough to hold all the pickles.
3. Add pickles to the egg wash and stir well to coat.
4. Place breadcrumbs in a large plastic bag or container with lid.
5. Drain egg wash from pickles and place them in bag with breadcrumbs. Shake to coat.
6. Pile pickles into air fryer basket and spray with oil.
7. Cook for 5minutes. Shake basket and spray with oil.
8. Cook 5 more minutes. Shake and spray again. Separate any pickles that have stuck together and mist any spots you've missed.
9. Cook for 5minutes longer or until dark golden brown and crispy.

Cinnamon Pita Chips

Servings: 4

Cooking Time: 6 Minutes

Ingredients:

- 2 tablespoons sugar
- 2 teaspoons cinnamon
- 2 whole 6-inch pitas, whole grain or white
- oil for misting or cooking spray

Directions:

1. Mix sugar and cinnamon together.
2. Cut each pita in half and each half into 4 wedges. Break apart each wedge at the fold.
3. Mist one side of pita wedges with oil or cooking spray. Sprinkle them all with half of the cinnamon sugar.
4. Turn the wedges over, mist the other side with oil or cooking spray, and sprinkle with the remaining cinnamon sugar.
5. Place pita wedges in air fryer basket and cook at 330°F for 2minutes.
6. Shake basket and cook 2 more minutes. Shake again, and if needed cook 2 more minutes, until crisp. Watch carefully because at this point they will cook very quickly.

Root Vegetable Crisps

Servings: 4

Cooking Time: 8 Minutes

Ingredients:

➢ 1 small taro root, peeled and washed

➢ 1 small yucca root, peeled and washed

➢ 1 small purple sweet potato, washed

➢ 2 cups filtered water

➢ 2 teaspoons extra-virgin olive oil

➢ ½ teaspoon salt

Directions:

1. Using a mandolin, slice the taro root, yucca root, and purple sweet potato into ⅛-inch slices.

2. Add the water to a large bowl. Add the sliced vegetables and soak for at least 30 minutes.

3. Preheat the air fryer to 370°F.

4. Drain the water and pat the vegetables dry with a paper towel or kitchen cloth. Toss the vegetables with the olive oil and sprinkle with salt. Liberally spray the air fryer basket with olive oil mist.

5. Place the vegetables into the air fryer basket, making sure not to overlap the pieces.

6. Cook for 8 minutes, shaking the basket every 2 minutes, until the outer edges start to turn up and the vegetables start to brown. Remove from the basket and serve warm. Repeat with the remaining vegetable slices until all are cooked.

Cheesy Pigs In A Blanket

Servings: 4

Cooking Time: 7 Minutes

Ingredients:

- ➢ 24 cocktail size smoked sausages
- ➢ 6 slices deli-sliced Cheddar cheese, each cut into 8 rectangular pieces
- ➢ 1 (8-ounce) tube refrigerated crescent roll dough
- ➢ ketchup or mustard for dipping

Directions:

1. Unroll the crescent roll dough into one large sheet. If your crescent roll dough has perforated seams, pinch or roll all the perforated seams together. Cut the large sheet of dough into 4 rectangles. Then cut each rectangle into 6 pieces by making one slice lengthwise in the middle and 2 slices horizontally. You should have 24 pieces of dough.

2. Make a deep slit lengthwise down the center of the cocktail sausage. Stuff two pieces of cheese into the slit in the sausage. Roll one piece of crescent dough around the stuffed cocktail sausage leaving the ends of the sausage exposed. Pinch the seam together. Repeat with the remaining sausages.

3. Preheat the air fryer to 350°F.

4. Air-fry in 2 batches, placing the sausages seam side down in the basket. Air-fry for 7 minutes. Serve hot with ketchup or your favorite mustard for dipping.

Fried Cheese Ravioli With Marinara Sauce

Servings: 4

Cooking Time: 7 Minutes

Ingredients:

➢ 1 pound cheese ravioli, fresh or frozen

➢ 2 eggs, lightly beaten

➢ 1 cup plain breadcrumbs

➢ ½ teaspoon paprika

➢ ½ teaspoon dried oregano

➢ ½ teaspoon salt

➢ grated Parmesan cheese

➢ chopped fresh parsley

➢ 1 to 2 cups marinara sauce (jarred or homemade)

Directions:

1. Bring a stockpot of salted water to a boil. Boil the ravioli according to the package directions and then drain. Let the cooked ravioli cool to a temperature where you can comfortably handle them.

2. While the pasta is cooking, set up a dredging station with two shallow dishes. Place the eggs into one dish. Combine the breadcrumbs, paprika, dried oregano and salt in the other dish.

3. Preheat the air fryer to 380°F.

4. Working with one at a time, dip the cooked ravioli into the egg, coating all sides. Then press the ravioli into the breadcrumbs, making sure that all sides are covered. Transfer the ravioli to the air fryer basket, cooking in batches, one layer at a time. Air-fry at 380°F for 7 minutes.

5. While the ravioli is air-frying, bring the marinara sauce to a simmer on the stovetop. Transfer to a small bowl.

6. Sprinkle a little Parmesan cheese and chopped parsley on top of the fried ravioli and serve warm with the marinara sauce on the side for dipping.

Parmesan Pizza Nuggets

| Servings: 8 | Cooking Time: 6 Minutes |

Ingredients:

- ¾ cup warm filtered water
- 1 package fast-rising yeast
- ½ teaspoon salt
- 2 cups all-purpose flour
- ¼ cup finely grated Parmesan cheese
- 1 teaspoon Italian seasoning
- 2 tablespoon extra-virgin olive oil
- 1 teaspoon kosher salt

Directions:

1. Preheat the air fryer to 370°F.

2. In a large microwave-safe bowl, add the water. Heat for 40 seconds in the microwave. Remove and mix in the yeast and salt. Let sit 5 minutes.

3. Meanwhile, in a medium bowl, mix the flour with the Parmesan cheese and Italian seasoning. Set aside.

4. Using a stand mixer with a dough hook attachment, add the yeast liquid and then mix in the flour mixture ⅓ cup at a time until all the flour mixture is added and a dough is formed.

5. Remove the bowl from the stand, and then let the dough rise for 1 hour in a warm space, covered with a kitchen towel.

6. After the dough has doubled in size, remove it from the bowl and punch it down a few times on a lightly floured flat surface.

7. Divide the dough into 4 balls, and then roll each ball out into a long, skinny, sticklike shape.

8. Using a sharp knife, cut each dough stick into 6 pieces. Repeat for the remaining dough balls until you have about 24 nuggets formed.

9. Lightly brush the top of each bite with the egg whites and cover with a pinch of sea salt.

10. Spray the air fryer basket with olive oil spray and place the pizza nuggets on top. Cook for 6 minutes, or until lightly browned. Remove and keep warm.

11. Repeat until all the nuggets are cooked.

12. Serve warm.

Bagel Chips

Servings: 2

Cooking Time: 4 Minutes

Ingredients:

- ➤ Sweet
- ➤ 1 large plain bagel
- ➤ 2 teaspoons sugar
- ➤ 1 teaspoon ground cinnamon
- ➤ butter-flavored cooking spray
- ➤ Savory
- ➤ 1 large plain bagel
- ➤ 1 teaspoon Italian seasoning
- ➤ ½ teaspoon garlic powder
- ➤ oil for misting or cooking spray

Directions:

1. Preheat air fryer to 390°F.

2. Cut bagel into ¼-inch slices or thinner.

3. Mix the seasonings together.

4. Spread out the slices, mist with oil or cooking spray, and sprinkle with half of the seasonings.

5. Turn over and repeat to coat the other side with oil or cooking spray and seasonings.

6. Place in air fryer basket and cook for 2minutes. Shake basket or stir a little and continue cooking for 2 minutes or until toasty brown and crispy.

Crispy Spiced Chickpeas

Servings: 2

Cooking Time: 20 Minutes

Ingredients:

- ➢ 1 (15-ounce) can chickpeas, drained (or 1½ cups cooked chickpeas)
- ➢ ½ teaspoon salt
- ➢ ½ teaspoon chili powder
- ➢ ¼ teaspoon ground cinnamon
- ➢ ⅛ teaspoon smoked paprika
- ➢ pinch ground cayenne pepper
- ➢ 1 tablespoon olive oil

Directions:

1. Preheat the air fryer to 400°F.

2. Dry the chickpeas as well as you can with a clean kitchen towel, rubbing off any loose skins as necessary. Combine the spices in a small bowl. Toss the chickpeas with the olive oil and then add the spices and toss again.

3. Air-fry for 15 minutes, shaking the basket a couple of times while they cook.

4. Check the chickpeas to see if they are crispy enough and if necessary, air-fry for another 5 minutes to crisp them further. Serve warm, or cool to room temperature and store in an airtight container for up to two weeks.

Sausage And Cheese Rolls

Servings: 3

Cooking Time: 18 Minutes

Ingredients:

➢ 3 3- to 3½-ounce sweet or hot Italian sausage links

➢ 2 1-ounce string cheese stick(s), unwrapped and cut in half lengthwise

➢ Three quarters from one thawed sheet (cut the sheet into four quarters; wrap and refreeze one of them) A 17.25-ounce box frozen puff pastry

Directions:

1. Preheat the air fryer to 400°F.

2. When the machine is at temperature, set the sausage links in the basket and air-fry undisturbed for 12 minutes, or until cooked through.

3. Use kitchen tongs to transfer the links to a wire rack. Cool for 15 minutes. (If necessary, pour out any rendered fat that has collected below the basket in the machine.)

4. Cut the sausage links in half lengthwise. Sandwich half a string cheese stick between two sausage halves, trimming the ends so the cheese doesn't stick out beyond the meat.

5. Roll each piece of puff pastry into a 6 x 6-inch square on a clean, dry work surface. Set the sausage-cheese sandwich at one edge and roll it up in the dough. The ends will be open like a pig-in-a-blanket. Repeat with the remaining puff pastry, sausage, and cheese.

6. Set the rolls seam side down in the basket. Air-fry undisturbed for 6 minutes, or until puffed and golden brown.

7. Use a nonstick-safe spatula, and perhaps a flatware fork for balance, to transfer the rolls to a wire rack. Cool for at least 5 minutes before serving.

Blistered Shishito Peppers

Servings: 3

Cooking Time: 5 Minutes

Ingredients:

➢ 6 ounces (about 18) Shishito peppers

➢ Vegetable oil spray

➢ For garnishing Coarse sea or kosher salt and lemon wedges

Directions:

1. Preheat the air fryer to 400°F.

2. Put the peppers in a bowl and lightly coat them with vegetable oil spray. Toss gently, spray again, and toss until the peppers are glistening but not drenched.

3. Pour the peppers into the basket, spread them into as close to one layer as you can, and air-fry for 5 minutes, tossing and rearranging the peppers at the 2- and 4-minute marks, until the peppers are blistered and even blackened in spots.

4. Pour the peppers into a bowl, add salt to taste, and toss gently. Serve the peppers with lemon wedges to squeeze over them.

VEGETARIANS RECIPES

Roasted Vegetable Lasagna

Servings: 6   Cooking Time: 55 Minutes

Ingredients:

- 1 zucchini, sliced
- 1 yellow squash, sliced
- 8 ounces mushrooms, sliced
- 1 red bell pepper, cut into 2-inch strips
- 1 tablespoon olive oil
- 2 cups ricotta cheese
- 2 cups grated mozzarella cheese, divided
- 1 egg
- 1 teaspoon salt
- freshly ground black pepper
- ¼ cup shredded carrots

- ½ cup chopped fresh spinach
- 8 lasagna noodles, cooked
- Béchamel Sauce:
- 3 tablespoons butter
- 3 tablespoons flour
- 2½ cups milk
- ½ cup grated Parmesan cheese
- ½ teaspoon salt
- freshly ground black pepper
- pinch of ground nutmeg

Directions:

1. Preheat the air fryer to 400°F.

2. Toss the zucchini, yellow squash, mushrooms and red pepper in a large bowl with the olive oil and season with salt and pepper. Air-fry for 10 minutes, shaking the basket once or twice while the vegetables cook.

3. While the vegetables are cooking, make the béchamel sauce and cheese filling. Melt the butter in a medium saucepan over medium-high heat on the stovetop. Add the flour and whisk, cooking for a couple of minutes. Add the milk and whisk vigorously until smooth. Bring the mixture to a boil and simmer until the sauce thickens. Stir in the Parmesan cheese and season with the salt, pepper and nutmeg. Set the sauce aside.

4. Combine the ricotta cheese, 1¼ cups of the mozzarella cheese, egg, salt and pepper in a large bowl and stir until combined. Fold in the carrots and spinach.

5. When the vegetables have finished cooking, build the lasagna. Use a baking dish that is 6 inches in diameter and 4 inches high. Cover the bottom of the baking dish with a little béchamel sauce. Top with two lasagna noodles, cut to fit the dish and overlapping each other a little. Spoon a third of the ricotta cheese mixture and then a third of the roasted veggies on top of the noodles. Pour ½ cup of béchamel sauce on top and then repeat these layers two more times: noodles – cheese mixture – vegetables – béchamel sauce. Sprinkle the remaining mozzarella cheese over the top. Cover the dish with aluminum foil, tenting it loosely so the aluminum doesn't touch the cheese.

6. Lower the dish into the air fryer basket using an aluminum foil sling (fold a piece of aluminum foil into a strip about 2-inches wide by 24-inches long). Fold the ends of the aluminum foil over the top of the dish before returning the basket to the air fryer. Air-fry for 45 minutes, removing the foil for the last 2 minutes, to slightly brown the cheese on top.

7. Let the lasagna rest for at least 20 minutes to set up a little before slicing into it and serving.

Asparagus, Mushroom And Cheese Soufflés

Servings: 3   Cooking Time: 21 Minutes

Ingredients:

- butter
- grated Parmesan cheese
- 3 button mushrooms, thinly sliced
- 8 spears asparagus, sliced ½-inch long
- 1 teaspoon olive oil
- 1 tablespoon butter
- 4½ teaspoons flour

- pinch paprika
- pinch ground nutmeg
- salt and freshly ground black pepper
- ½ cup milk
- ½ cup grated Gruyère cheese or other Swiss cheese (about 2 ounces)
- 2 eggs, separated

Directions:

1. Butter three 6-ounce ramekins and dust with grated Parmesan cheese. (Butter the ramekins and then coat the butter with Parmesan by shaking it around in the ramekin and dumping out any excess.)

2. Preheat the air fryer to 400°F.

3. Toss the mushrooms and asparagus in a bowl with the olive oil. Transfer the vegetables to the air fryer and air-fry for 7 minutes, shaking the basket once or twice to redistribute the Ingredients while they cook.

4. While the vegetables are cooking, make the soufflé base. Melt the butter in a saucepan on the stovetop over medium heat. Add the flour, stir and cook for a minute or two. Add the paprika, nutmeg, salt and pepper. Whisk in the milk and bring the mixture to a simmer to thicken. Remove the pan from the heat and add the cheese, stirring to melt. Let the mixture cool for just a few minutes and then whisk the egg yolks in, one at a time. Stir in the cooked mushrooms and asparagus. Let this soufflé base cool.

5. In a separate bowl, whisk the egg whites to soft peak stage (the point at which the whites can almost stand up on the end of your whisk). Fold the whipped egg whites into the soufflé base, adding a little at a time.

6. Preheat the air fryer to 330°F.

7. Transfer the batter carefully to the buttered ramekins, leaving about ½-inch at the top. Place the ramekins into the air fryer basket and air-fry for 14 minutes. The soufflés should have risen nicely and be brown on top. Serve immediately.

Veggie Burgers

Servings: 4

Cooking Time: 15 Minutes

Ingredients:

➢ 2 cans black beans, rinsed and drained

➢ ½ cup cooked quinoa

➢ ½ cup shredded raw sweet potato

➢ ¼ cup diced red onion

➢ 2 teaspoons ground cumin

➢ 1 teaspoon coriander powder

➢ ½ teaspoon salt

➢ oil for misting or cooking spray

➢ 8 slices bread

➢ suggested toppings: lettuce, tomato, red onion, Pepper Jack cheese, guacamole

Directions:

1. In a medium bowl, mash the beans with a fork.

2. Add the quinoa, sweet potato, onion, cumin, coriander, and salt and mix well with the fork.

3. Shape into 4 patties, each ¾-inch thick.

4. Mist both sides with oil or cooking spray and also mist the basket.

5. Cook at 390°F for 15minutes.

6. Follow the recipe for Toast, Plain & Simple.

7. Pop the veggie burgers back in the air fryer for a minute or two to reheat if necessary.

8. Serve on the toast with your favorite burger toppings.

Thai Peanut Veggie Burgers

Servings: 6   Cooking Time: 14 Minutes

Ingredients:

- One 15.5-ounce can cannellini beans
- 1 teaspoon minced garlic
- ¼ cup chopped onion
- 1 Thai chili pepper, sliced
- 2 tablespoons natural peanut butter
- ½ teaspoon black pepper
- ½ teaspoon salt
- ⅓ cup all-purpose flour (optional)

- ½ cup cooked quinoa
- 1 large carrot, grated
- 1 cup shredded red cabbage
- ¼ cup peanut dressing
- ¼ cup chopped cilantro
- 6 Hawaiian rolls
- 6 butterleaf lettuce leaves

Directions:

1. Preheat the air fryer to 350°F.

2. To a blender or food processor fitted with a metal blade, add the beans, garlic, onion, chili pepper, peanut butter, pepper, and salt. Pulse for 5 to 10 seconds. Do not over process. The mixture should be coarse, not smooth.

3. Remove from the blender or food processor and spoon into a large bowl. Mix in the cooked quinoa and carrots. At this point, the mixture should begin to hold together to form small patties. If the dough appears to be too sticky (meaning you likely processed a little too long), add the flour to hold the patties together.

4. Using a large spoon, form 8 equal patties out of the batter.

5. Liberally spray a metal trivet with olive oil spray and set in the air fryer basket. Place the patties into the basket, leaving enough space to be able to turn them with a spatula.

6. Cook for 7 minutes, flip, and cook another 7 minutes.

7. Remove from the heat and repeat with additional patties.

8. To serve, place the red cabbage in a bowl and toss with peanut dressing and cilantro. Place the veggie burger on a bun, and top with a slice of lettuce and cabbage slaw.

Egg Rolls

Servings: 4

Cooking Time: 8 Minutes

Ingredients:

- 1 clove garlic, minced
- 1 teaspoon sesame oil
- 1 teaspoon olive oil
- ½ cup chopped celery
- ½ cup grated carrots
- 2 green onions, chopped
- 2 ounces mushrooms, chopped
- 2 cups shredded Napa cabbage
- 1 teaspoon low-sodium soy sauce
- 1 teaspoon cornstarch
- salt
- 1 egg
- 1 tablespoon water
- 4 egg roll wraps
- olive oil for misting or cooking spray

Directions:

1. In a large skillet, sauté garlic in sesame and olive oils over medium heat for 1 minute.
2. Add celery, carrots, onions, and mushrooms to skillet. Cook 1 minute, stirring.
3. Stir in cabbage, cover, and cook for 1 minute or just until cabbage slightly wilts.
4. In a small bowl, mix soy sauce and cornstarch. Stir into vegetables to thicken. Remove from heat. Salt to taste if needed.
5. Beat together egg and water in a small bowl.
6. Divide filling into 4 portions and roll up in egg roll wraps. Brush all over with egg wash to seal.
7. Mist egg rolls very lightly with olive oil or cooking spray and place in air fryer basket.
8. Cook at 390°F for 4minutes. Turn over and cook 4 more minutes, until golden brown and crispy.

Roasted Vegetable, Brown Rice And Black Bean Burrito

Servings: 2

Cooking Time: 20 Minutes

Ingredients:

- ½ zucchini, sliced ¼-inch thick
- ½ red onion, sliced
- 1 yellow bell pepper, sliced
- 2 teaspoons olive oil
- salt and freshly ground black pepper
- 2 burrito size flour tortillas
- 1 cup grated pepper jack cheese
- ½ cup cooked brown rice
- ½ cup canned black beans, drained and rinsed
- ¼ teaspoon ground cumin
- 1 tablespoon chopped fresh cilantro
- fresh salsa, guacamole and sour cream, for serving

Directions:

1. Preheat the air fryer to 400°F.

2. Toss the vegetables in a bowl with the olive oil, salt and freshly ground black pepper. Air-fry at 400°F for 12 to 15 minutes, shaking the basket a few times during the cooking process. The vegetables are done when they are cooked to your liking.

3. In the meantime, start building the burritos. Lay the tortillas out on the counter. Sprinkle half of the cheese in the center of the tortillas. Combine the rice, beans, cumin and cilantro in a bowl, season to taste with salt and freshly ground black pepper and then divide the mixture between the two tortillas. When the vegetables have finished cooking, transfer them to the two tortillas, placing the vegetables on top of the rice and beans. Sprinkle the remaining cheese on top and then roll the burritos up, tucking in the sides of the tortillas as you roll. Brush or spray the outside of the burritos with olive oil and transfer them to the air fryer.

4. Air-fry at 360°F for 8 minutes, turning them over when there are about 2 minutes left. The burritos will have slightly brown spots, but will still be pliable.

5. Serve with some fresh salsa, guacamole and sour cream.

Cheesy Enchilada Stuffed Baked Potatoes

Servings: 4   Cooking Time: 37 Minutes

Ingredients:

➤ 2 medium russet potatoes, washed
➤ One 15-ounce can mild red enchilada sauce
➤ One 15-ounce can low-sodium black beans, rinsed and drained
➤ 1 teaspoon taco seasoning
➤ ½ cup shredded cheddar cheese
➤ 1 medium avocado, halved

➤ ½ teaspoon garlic powder
➤ ¼ teaspoon black pepper
➤ ¼ teaspoon salt
➤ 2 teaspoons fresh lime juice
➤ 2 tablespoon chopped red onion
➤ ¼ cup chopped cilantro

Directions:

1. Preheat the air fryer to 390°F.

2. Puncture the outer surface of the potatoes with a fork.

3. Set the potatoes inside the air fryer basket and cook for 20 minutes, rotate, and cook another 10 minutes.

4. In a large bowl, mix the enchilada sauce, black beans, and taco seasoning.

5. When the potatoes have finished cooking, carefully remove them from the air fryer basket and let cool for 5 minutes.

6. Using a pair of tongs to hold the potato if it's still too hot to touch, slice the potato in half lengthwise. Use a spoon to scoop out the potato flesh and add it into the bowl with the enchilada sauce. Mash the potatoes with the enchilada sauce mixture, creating a uniform stuffing.

7. Place the potato skins into an air-fryer-safe pan and stuff the halves with the enchilada stuffing. Sprinkle the cheese over the top of each potato.

8. Set the air fryer temperature to 350°F, return the pan to the air fryer basket, and cook for another 5 to 7 minutes to heat the potatoes and melt the cheese.

9. While the potatoes are cooking, take the avocado and scoop out the flesh into a small bowl. Mash it with the back of a fork; then mix in the garlic powder, pepper, salt, lime juice, and onion. Set aside.

10. When the potatoes have finished cooking, remove the pan from the air fryer and place the potato halves on a plate. Top with avocado mash and fresh cilantro. Serve immediately.

Vegetable Hand Pies

Servings: 8

Cooking Time: 10 Minutes Per Batch

Ingredients:

- ¾ cup vegetable broth
- 8 ounces potatoes
- ¾ cup frozen chopped broccoli, thawed
- ¼ cup chopped mushrooms
- 1 tablespoon cornstarch
- 1 tablespoon milk
- 1 can organic flaky biscuits (8 large biscuits)
- oil for misting or cooking spray

Directions:

1. Place broth in medium saucepan over low heat.

2. While broth is heating, grate raw potato into a bowl of water to prevent browning. You will need ¾ cup grated potato.

3. Roughly chop the broccoli.

4. Drain potatoes and put them in the broth along with the broccoli and mushrooms. Cook on low for 5 minutes.

5. Dissolve cornstarch in milk, then stir the mixture into the broth. Cook about a minute, until mixture thickens a little. Remove from heat and cool slightly.

6. Separate each biscuit into 2 rounds. Divide vegetable mixture evenly over half the biscuit rounds, mounding filling in the center of each.

7. Top the four rounds with filling, then the other four rounds and crimp the edges together with a fork.

8. Spray both sides with oil or cooking spray and place 4 pies in a single layer in the air fryer basket.

9. Cook at 330°F for approximately 10 minutes.

10. Repeat with the remaining biscuits. The second batch may cook more quickly because the fryer will be hot.

Mushroom And Fried Onion Quesadilla

Servings: 2

Cooking Time: 33 Minutes

Ingredients:

- ➤ 1 onion, sliced
- ➤ 2 tablespoons butter, melted
- ➤ 10 ounces button mushrooms, sliced
- ➤ 2 tablespoons Worcestershire sauce
- ➤ salt and freshly ground black pepper
- ➤ 4 (8-inch) flour tortillas
- ➤ 2 cups grated Fontina cheese
- ➤ vegetable or olive oil

Directions:

1. Preheat the air fryer to 400°F.

2. Toss the onion slices with the melted butter and transfer them to the air fryer basket. Air-fry at 400°F for 15 minutes, shaking the basket several times during the cooking process. Add the mushrooms and Worcestershire sauce to the onions and stir to combine. Air-fry at 400°F for an additional 10 minutes. Season with salt and freshly ground black pepper.

3. Lay two of the tortillas on a cutting board. Top each tortilla with ½ cup of the grated cheese, half of the onion and mushroom mixture and then finally another ½ cup of the cheese. Place the remaining tortillas on top of the cheese and press down firmly.

4. Brush the air fryer basket with a little oil. Place a quesadilla in the basket and brush the top with a little oil. Secure the top tortilla to the bottom with three toothpicks and air-fry at 400°F for 5 minutes. Flip the quesadilla over by inverting it onto a plate and sliding it back into the basket. Remove the toothpicks and brush the other side with oil. Air-fry for an additional 3 minutes.

5. Invert the quesadilla onto a cutting board and cut it into 4 or 6 triangles. Serve immediately.

Stuffed Zucchini Boats

Servings: 2   Cooking Time: 20 Minutes

Ingredients:

- olive oil
- ½ cup onion, finely chopped
- 1 clove garlic, finely minced
- ½ teaspoon dried oregano
- ¼ teaspoon dried thyme
- ¾ cup couscous
- 1½ cups chicken stock, divided
- 1 tomato, seeds removed and finely chopped
- ½ cup coarsely chopped Kalamata olives

- ½ cup grated Romano cheese
- ¼ cup pine nuts, toasted
- 1 tablespoon chopped fresh parsley
- 1 teaspoon salt
- freshly ground black pepper
- 1 egg, beaten
- 1 cup grated mozzarella cheese, divided
- 2 thick zucchini

Directions:

1. Preheat a sauté pan on the stovetop over medium-high heat. Add the olive oil and sauté the onion until it just starts to soften–about 4 minutes. Stir in the garlic, dried oregano and thyme. Add the couscous and sauté for just a minute. Add 1¼ cups of the chicken stock and simmer over low heat for 3 to 5 minutes, until liquid has been absorbed and the couscous is soft. Remove the pan from heat and set it aside to cool slightly.

2. Fluff the couscous and add the tomato, Kalamata olives, Romano cheese, pine nuts, parsley, salt and pepper. Mix well. Add the remaining chicken stock, the egg and ½ cup of the mozzarella cheese. Stir to ensure everything is combined.

3. Cut each zucchini in half lengthwise. Then, trim each half of the zucchini into four 5-inch lengths. (Save the trimmed ends of the zucchini for another use.) Use a spoon to scoop out the center of the zucchini, leaving some flesh around the sides. Brush both sides of the zucchini with olive oil and season the cut side with salt and pepper.

4. Preheat the air fryer to 380°F.

5. Divide the couscous filling between the four zucchini boats. Use your hands to press the filling together and fill the inside of the zucchini. The filling should be mounded into the boats and rounded on top.

6. Transfer the zucchini boats to the air fryer basket and drizzle the stuffed zucchini boats with olive oil. Air-fry for 19 minutes. Then, sprinkle the remaining mozzarella cheese on top of the zucchini, pressing it down onto the filling lightly to prevent it from blowing around in the air fryer. Air-fry for one more minute to melt the cheese. Transfer the finished zucchini boats to a serving platter and garnish with the chopped parsley.

SANDWICHES AND BURGERS RECIPES

Best-ever Roast Beef Sandwiches

Servings: 6

Cooking Time: 30-50 Minutes

Ingredients:

➤ 2½ teaspoons Olive oil
➤ 1½ teaspoons Dried oregano
➤ 1½ teaspoons Dried thyme
➤ 1½ teaspoons Onion powder
➤ 1½ teaspoons Table salt
➤ 1½ teaspoons Ground black pepper
➤ 3 pounds Beef eye of round
➤ 6 Round soft rolls, such as Kaiser rolls or hamburger buns (gluten-free, if a concern), split open lengthwise
➤ ¾ cup Regular, low-fat, or fat-free mayonnaise (gluten-free, if a concern)
➤ 6 Romaine lettuce leaves, rinsed
➤ 6 Round tomato slices (¼ inch thick)

Directions:

1. Preheat the air fryer to 350°F .

2. Mix the oil, oregano, thyme, onion powder, salt, and pepper in a small bowl. Spread this mixture all over the eye of round.

3. When the machine is at temperature, set the beef in the basket and air-fry for 30 to 50 minutes (the range depends on the size of the cut), turning the meat twice, until an instant-read meat thermometer inserted into the thickest piece of the meat registers 130°F for rare, 140°F for medium, or 150°F for well-done.

4. Use kitchen tongs to transfer the beef to a cutting board. Cool for 10 minutes. If serving now, carve into ⅛-inch-thick slices. Spread each roll with 2 tablespoons mayonnaise and divide the beef slices between the rolls. Top with a lettuce leaf and a tomato slice and serve. Or set the beef in a container, cover, and refrigerate for up to 3 days to make cold roast beef sandwiches anytime.

Eggplant Parmesan Subs

Servings: 2

Cooking Time: 13 Minutes

Ingredients:

➢ 4 Peeled eggplant slices (about ½ inch thick and 3 inches in diameter)

➢ Olive oil spray

➢ 2 tablespoons plus 2 teaspoons Jarred pizza sauce, any variety except creamy

➢ ¼ cup (about ⅔ ounce) Finely grated Parmesan cheese

➢ 2 Small, long soft rolls, such as hero, hoagie, or Italian sub rolls (gluten-free, if a concern), split open lengthwise

Directions:

1. Preheat the air fryer to 350°F .

2. When the machine is at temperature, coat both sides of the eggplant slices with olive oil spray. Set them in the basket in one layer and air-fry undisturbed for 10 minutes, until lightly browned and softened.

3. Increase the machine's temperature to 375°F (or 370°F, if that's the closest setting—unless the machine is already at 360°F, in which case leave it alone). Top each eggplant slice with 2 teaspoons pizza sauce, then 1 tablespoon cheese. Air-fry undisturbed for 2 minutes, or until the cheese has melted.

4. Use a nonstick-safe spatula, and perhaps a flatware fork for balance, to transfer the eggplant slices cheese side up to a cutting board. Set the roll(s) cut side down in the basket in one layer (working in batches as necessary) and air-fry undisturbed for 1 minute, to toast the rolls a bit and warm them up. Set 2 eggplant slices in each warm roll.

Inside Out Cheeseburgers

Servings: 2

Cooking Time: 20 Minutes

Ingredients:

- ¾ pound lean ground beef
- 3 tablespoons minced onion
- 4 teaspoons ketchup
- 2 teaspoons yellow mustard
- salt and freshly ground black pepper
- 4 slices of Cheddar cheese, broken into smaller pieces
- 8 hamburger dill pickle chips

Directions:

1. Combine the ground beef, minced onion, ketchup, mustard, salt and pepper in a large bowl. Mix well to thoroughly combine the ingredients. Divide the meat into four equal portions.

2. To make the stuffed burgers, flatten each portion of meat into a thin patty. Place 4 pickle chips and half of the cheese onto the center of two of the patties, leaving a rim around the edge of the patty exposed. Place the remaining two patties on top of the first and press the meat together firmly, sealing the edges tightly. With the burgers on a flat surface, press the sides of the burger with the palm of your hand to create a straight edge. This will help keep the stuffing inside the burger while it cooks.

3. Preheat the air fryer to 370°F.

4. Place the burgers inside the air fryer basket and air-fry for 20 minutes, flipping the burgers over halfway through the cooking time.

5. Serve the cheeseburgers on buns with lettuce and tomato.

Philly Cheesesteak Sandwiches

Servings: 3

Cooking Time: 9 Minutes

Ingredients:

➢ ¾ pound Shaved beef

➢ 1 tablespoon Worcestershire sauce (gluten-free, if a concern)

➢ ¼ teaspoon Garlic powder

➢ ¼ teaspoon Mild paprika

➢ 6 tablespoons (1½ ounces) Frozen bell pepper strips (do not thaw)

➢ 2 slices, broken into rings Very thin yellow or white medium onion slice(s)

➢ 6 ounces (6 to 8 slices) Provolone cheese slices

➢ 3 Long soft rolls such as hero, hoagie, or Italian sub rolls, or hot dog buns (gluten-free, if a concern), split open lengthwise

Directions:

1. Preheat the air fryer to 400°F.

2. When the machine is at temperature, spread the shaved beef in the basket, leaving a ½-inch perimeter around the meat for good air flow. Sprinkle the meat with the Worcestershire sauce, paprika, and garlic powder. Spread the peppers and onions on top of the meat.

3. Air-fry undisturbed for 6 minutes, or until cooked through. Set the cheese on top of the meat. Continue air-frying undisturbed for 3 minutes, or until the cheese has melted.

4. Use kitchen tongs to divide the meat and cheese layers in the basket between the rolls or buns. Serve hot.

Inside-out Cheeseburgers

Servings: 3

Cooking Time: 9-11 Minutes

Ingredients:

➤ 1 pound 2 ounces 90% lean ground beef

➤ ¾ teaspoon Dried oregano

➤ ¾ teaspoon Table salt

➤ ¾ teaspoon Ground black pepper

➤ ¼ teaspoon Garlic powder

➤ 6 tablespoons (about 1½ ounces) Shredded Cheddar, Swiss, or other semi-firm cheese, or a purchased blend of shredded cheeses

➤ 3 Hamburger buns (gluten-free, if a concern), split open

Directions:

1. Preheat the air fryer to 375°F .

2. Gently mix the ground beef, oregano, salt, pepper, and garlic powder in a bowl until well combined without turning the mixture to mush. Form it into two 6-inch patties for the small batch, three for the medium, or four for the large.

3. Place 2 tablespoons of the shredded cheese in the center of each patty. With clean hands, fold the sides of the patty up to cover the cheese, then pick it up and roll it gently into a ball to seal the cheese inside. Gently press it back into a 5-inch burger without letting any cheese squish out. Continue filling and preparing more burgers, as needed.

4. Place the burgers in the basket in one layer and air-fry undisturbed for 8 minutes for medium or 10 minutes for well-done. (An instant-read meat thermometer won't work for these burgers because it will hit the mostly melted cheese inside and offer a hotter temperature than the surrounding meat.)

5. Use a nonstick-safe spatula, and perhaps a flatware fork for balance, to transfer the burgers to a cutting board. Set the buns cut side down in the basket in one layer (working in batches as necessary) and air-fry undisturbed for 1 minute, to toast a bit and warm up. Cool the burgers a few minutes more, then serve them warm in the buns.

Asian Glazed Meatballs

Servings: 4

Cooking Time: 10 Minutes

Ingredients:

- ➢ 1 large shallot, finely chopped
- ➢ 2 cloves garlic, minced
- ➢ 1 tablespoon grated fresh ginger
- ➢ 2 teaspoons fresh thyme, finely chopped
- ➢ 1½ cups brown mushrooms, very finely chopped (a food processor works well here)
- ➢ 2 tablespoons soy sauce
- ➢ freshly ground black pepper
- ➢ 1 pound ground beef
- ➢ ½ pound ground pork
- ➢ 3 egg yolks
- ➢ 1 cup Thai sweet chili sauce (spring roll sauce)
- ➢ ¼ cup toasted sesame seeds
- ➢ 2 scallions, sliced

Directions:

1. Combine the shallot, garlic, ginger, thyme, mushrooms, soy sauce, freshly ground black pepper, ground beef and pork, and egg yolks in a bowl and mix the ingredients together. Gently shape the mixture into 24 balls, about the size of a golf ball.

2. Preheat the air fryer to 380°F.

3. Working in batches, air-fry the meatballs for 8 minutes, turning the meatballs over halfway through the cooking time. Drizzle some of the Thai sweet chili sauce on top of each meatball and return the basket to the air fryer, air-frying for another 2 minutes. Reserve the remaining Thai sweet chili sauce for serving.

4. As soon as the meatballs are done, sprinkle with toasted sesame seeds and transfer them to a serving platter. Scatter the scallions around and serve warm.

Salmon Burgers

Servings: 3

Cooking Time: 8 Minutes

Ingredients:

- 1 pound 2 ounces Skinless salmon fillet, preferably fattier Atlantic salmon
- 1½ tablespoons Minced chives or the green part of a scallion
- ½ cup Plain panko bread crumbs (gluten-free, if a concern)
- 1½ teaspoons Dijon mustard (gluten-free, if a concern)
- 1½ teaspoons Drained and rinsed capers, minced
- 1½ teaspoons Lemon juice
- ¼ teaspoon Table salt
- ¼ teaspoon Ground black pepper
- Vegetable oil spray

Directions:

1. Preheat the air fryer to 375°F .

2. Cut the salmon into pieces that will fit in a food processor. Cover and pulse until coarsely chopped. Add the chives and pulse to combine, until the fish is ground but not a paste. Scrape down and remove the blade. Scrape the salmon mixture into a bowl. Add the bread crumbs, mustard, capers, lemon juice, salt, and pepper. Stir gently until well combined.

3. Use clean and dry hands to form the mixture into two 5-inch patties for a small batch, three 5-inch patties for a medium batch, or four 5-inch patties for a large one.

4. Coat both sides of each patty with vegetable oil spray. Set them in the basket in one layer and air-fry undisturbed for 8 minutes, or until browned and an instant-read meat thermometer inserted into the center of a burger registers 145°F.

5. Use a nonstick-safe spatula, and perhaps a flatware fork for balance, to transfer the burgers to a wire rack. Cool for 2 or 3 minutes before serving.

Reuben Sandwiches

Servings: 2

Cooking Time: 11 Minutes

Ingredients:

- ½ pound Sliced deli corned beef
- 4 teaspoons Regular or low-fat mayonnaise (not fat-free)
- 4 Rye bread slices
- 2 tablespoons plus 2 teaspoons Russian dressing
- ½ cup Purchased sauerkraut, squeezed by the handful over the sink to get rid of excess moisture
- 2 ounces (2 to 4 slices) Swiss cheese slices (optional)

Directions:

1. Set the corned beef in the basket, slip the basket into the machine, and heat the air fryer to 400°F. Air-fry undisturbed for 3 minutes from the time the basket is put in the machine, just to warm up the meat.

2. Use kitchen tongs to transfer the corned beef to a cutting board. Spread 1 teaspoon mayonnaise on one side of each slice of rye bread, rubbing the mayonnaise into the bread with a small flatware knife.

3. Place the bread slices mayonnaise side down on a cutting board. Spread the Russian dressing over the "dry" side of each slice. For one sandwich, top one slice of bread with the corned beef, sauerkraut, and cheese (if using). For two sandwiches, top two slices of bread each with half of the corned beef, sauerkraut, and cheese (if using). Close the sandwiches with the remaining bread, setting it mayonnaise side up on top.

4. Set the sandwich(es) in the basket and air-fry undisturbed for 8 minutes, or until browned and crunchy.

5. Use a nonstick-safe spatula, and perhaps a flatware fork for balance, to transfer the sandwich(es) to a cutting board. Cool for 2 or 3 minutes before slicing in half and serving.

Chicken Saltimbocca Sandwiches

Servings: 3

Cooking Time: 11 Minutes

Ingredients:

➤ 3 5- to 6-ounce boneless skinless chicken breasts

➤ 6 Thin prosciutto slices

➤ 6 Provolone cheese slices

➤ 3 Long soft rolls, such as hero, hoagie, or Italian sub rolls (gluten-free, if a concern), split open lengthwise

➤ 3 tablespoons Pesto, purchased or homemade (see the headnote)

Directions:

1. Preheat the air fryer to 400°F.

2. Wrap each chicken breast with 2 prosciutto slices, spiraling the prosciutto around the breast and overlapping the slices a bit to cover the breast. The prosciutto will stick to the chicken more readily than bacon does.

3. When the machine is at temperature, set the wrapped chicken breasts in the basket and air-fry undisturbed for 10 minutes, or until the prosciutto is frizzled and the chicken is cooked through.

4. Overlap 2 cheese slices on each breast. Air-fry undisturbed for 1 minute, or until melted. Take the basket out of the machine.

5. Smear the insides of the rolls with the pesto, then use kitchen tongs to put a wrapped and cheesy chicken breast in each roll.

Mexican Cheeseburgers

Servings: 4

Cooking Time: 22 Minutes

Ingredients:

- 1¼ pounds ground beef
- ¼ cup finely chopped onion
- ½ cup crushed yellow corn tortilla chips
- 1 (1.25-ounce) packet taco seasoning
- ¼ cup canned diced green chilies
- 1 egg, lightly beaten
- 4 ounces pepper jack cheese, grated
- 4 (12-inch) flour tortillas
- shredded lettuce, sour cream, guacamole, salsa (for topping)

Directions:

1. Combine the ground beef, minced onion, crushed tortilla chips, taco seasoning, green chilies, and egg in a large bowl. Mix thoroughly until combined – your hands are good tools for this. Divide the meat into four equal portions and shape each portion into an oval-shaped burger.

2. Preheat the air fryer to 370°F.

3. Air-fry the burgers for 18 minutes, turning them over halfway through the cooking time. Divide the cheese between the burgers, lower fryer to 340°F and air-fry for an additional 4 minutes to melt the cheese. (This will give you a burger that is medium-well. If you prefer your cheeseburger medium-rare, shorten the cooking time to about 15 minutes and then add the cheese and proceed with the recipe.)

4. While the burgers are cooking, warm the tortillas wrapped in aluminum foil in a 350°F oven, or in a skillet with a little oil over medium-high heat for a couple of minutes. Keep the tortillas warm until the burgers are ready.

5. To assemble the burgers, spread sour cream over three quarters of the tortillas and top each with some shredded lettuce and salsa. Place the Mexican cheeseburgers on the lettuce and top with guacamole. Fold the tortillas around the burger, starting with the bottom and then folding the sides in over the top. (A little sour cream can help hold the seam of the tortilla together.) Serve immediately.

Provolone Stuffed Meatballs

Servings: 4

Cooking Time: 12 Minutes

Ingredients:

➤ 1 tablespoon olive oil

➤ 1 small onion, very finely chopped

➤ 1 to 2 cloves garlic, minced

➤ ¾ pound ground beef

➤ ¾ pound ground pork

➤ ¾ cup breadcrumbs

➤ ¼ cup grated Parmesan cheese

➤ ¼ cup finely chopped fresh parsley (or 1 tablespoon dried parsley)

➤ ½ teaspoon dried oregano

➤ 1½ teaspoons salt

➤ freshly ground black pepper

➤ 2 eggs, lightly beaten

➤ 5 ounces sharp or aged provolone cheese, cut into 1-inch cubes

Directions:

1. Preheat a skillet over medium-high heat. Add the oil and cook the onion and garlic until tender, but not browned.

2. Transfer the onion and garlic to a large bowl and add the beef, pork, breadcrumbs, Parmesan cheese, parsley, oregano, salt, pepper and eggs. Mix well until all the ingredients are combined. Divide the mixture into 12 evenly sized balls. Make one meatball at a time, by pressing a hole in the meatball mixture with your finger and pushing a piece of provolone cheese into the hole. Mold the meat back into a ball, enclosing the cheese.

3. Preheat the air fryer to 380°F.

4. Working in two batches, transfer six of the meatballs to the air fryer basket and air-fry for 12 minutes, shaking the basket and turning the meatballs a couple of times during the cooking process. Repeat with the remaining six meatballs. You can pop the first batch of meatballs into the air fryer for the last two minutes of cooking to re-heat them. Serve warm.

Sausage And Pepper Heros

Servings: 3

Cooking Time: 11 Minutes

Ingredients:

- 3 links (about 9 ounces total) Sweet Italian sausages (gluten-free, if a concern)
- 1½ Medium red or green bell pepper(s), stemmed, cored, and cut into ½-inch-wide strips
- 1 medium Yellow or white onion(s), peeled, halved, and sliced into thin half-moons
- 3 Long soft rolls, such as hero, hoagie, or Italian sub rolls (gluten-free, if a concern), split open lengthwise
- For garnishing Balsamic vinegar
- For garnishing Fresh basil leaves

Directions:

1. Preheat the air fryer to 400°F.

2. When the machine is at temperature, set the sausage links in the basket in one layer and air-fry undisturbed for 5 minutes.

3. Add the pepper strips and onions. Continue air-frying, tossing and rearranging everything about once every minute, for 5 minutes, or until the sausages are browned and an instant-read meat thermometer inserted into one of the links registers 160°F.

4. Use a nonstick-safe spatula and kitchen tongs to transfer the sausages and vegetables to a cutting board. Set the rolls cut side down in the basket in one layer (working in batches as necessary) and air-fry undisturbed for 1 minute, to toast the rolls a bit and warm them up. Set 1 sausage with some pepper strips and onions in each warm roll, sprinkle balsamic vinegar over the sandwich fillings, and garnish with basil leaves.

FISH AND SEAFOOD RECIPES

Shrimp Sliders With Avocado

Servings: 4   Cooking Time: 10 Minutes

Ingredients:

- 16 raw jumbo shrimp, peeled, deveined and tails removed (about 1 pound)
- 1 rib celery, finely chopped
- 2 carrots, grated (about ½ cup) 2 teaspoons lemon juice
- 2 teaspoons Dijon mustard
- ¼ cup chopped fresh basil or parsley
- ½ cup breadcrumbs

- ½ teaspoon salt
- freshly ground black pepper
- vegetable or olive oil, in a spray bottle
- 8 slider buns
- mayonnaise
- butter lettuce
- 2 avocados, sliced and peeled

Directions:

1. Put the shrimp into a food processor and pulse it a few times to rough chop the shrimp. Remove three quarters of the shrimp and transfer it to a bowl. Continue to process the remaining shrimp in the food processor until it is a smooth purée. Transfer the purée to the bowl with the chopped shrimp.

2. Add the celery, carrots, lemon juice, mustard, basil, breadcrumbs, salt and pepper to the bowl and combine well.

3. Preheat the air fryer to 380°F.

4. While the air fryer Preheats, shape the shrimp mixture into 8 patties. Spray both sides of the patties with oil and transfer one layer of patties to the air fryer basket. Air-fry for 10 minutes, flipping the patties over halfway through the cooking time.

5. Prepare the slider rolls by toasting them and spreading a little mayonnaise on both halves. Place a piece of butter lettuce on the bottom bun, top with the shrimp slider and then finish with the avocado slices on top. Pop the top half of the bun on top and enjoy!

Lemon-roasted Salmon Fillets

Servings:3

Cooking Time: 7 Minutes

Ingredients:

- ➢ 3 6-ounce skin-on salmon fillets
- ➢ Olive oil spray
- ➢ 9 Very thin lemon slices
- ➢ ¾ teaspoon Ground black pepper
- ➢ ¼ teaspoon Table salt

Directions:

1. Preheat the air fryer to 400°F.

2. Generously coat the skin of each of the fillets with olive oil spray. Set the fillets skin side down on your work surface. Place three overlapping lemon slices down the length of each salmon fillet. Sprinkle them with the pepper and salt. Coat lightly with olive oil spray.

3. Use a nonstick-safe spatula to transfer the fillets one by one to the basket, leaving as much air space between them as possible. Air-fry undisturbed for 7 minutes, or until cooked through.

4. Use a nonstick-safe spatula to transfer the fillets to serving plates. Cool for only a minute or two before serving.

Sea Bass With Potato Scales And Caper Aïoli

Servings: 2

Cooking Time: 10 Minutes

Ingredients:

- 2 (6- to 8-ounce) fillets of sea bass
- salt and freshly ground black pepper
- ¼ cup mayonnaise
- 2 teaspoons finely chopped lemon zest
- 1 teaspoon chopped fresh thyme
- 2 fingerling potatoes, very thinly sliced into rounds
- olive oil
- ½ clove garlic, crushed into a paste
- 1 tablespoon capers, drained and rinsed
- 1 tablespoon olive oil
- 1 teaspoon lemon juice, to taste

Directions:

1. Preheat the air fryer to 400°F.

2. Season the fish well with salt and freshly ground black pepper. Mix the mayonnaise, lemon zest and thyme together in a small bowl. Spread a thin layer of the mayonnaise mixture on both fillets. Start layering rows of potato slices onto the fish fillets to simulate the fish scales. The second row should overlap the first row slightly. Dabbing a little more mayonnaise along the upper edge of the row of potatoes where the next row overlaps will help the potato slices stick. Press the potatoes onto the fish to secure them well and season again with salt. Brush or spray the potato layer with olive oil.

3. Transfer the fish to the air fryer and air-fry for 8 to 10 minutes, depending on the thickness of your fillets. 1-inch of fish should take 10 minutes at 400°F.

4. While the fish is cooking, add the garlic, capers, olive oil and lemon juice to the remaining mayonnaise mixture to make the caper aïoli.

5. Serve the fish warm with a dollop of the aïoli on top or on the side.

Maple Balsamic Glazed Salmon

Servings: 4

Cooking Time: 10 Minutes

Ingredients:

- ➢ 4 (6-ounce) fillets of salmon
- ➢ salt and freshly ground black pepper
- ➢ vegetable oil
- ➢ ¼ cup pure maple syrup
- ➢ 3 tablespoons balsamic vinegar
- ➢ 1 teaspoon Dijon mustard

Directions:

1. Preheat the air fryer to 400°F.

2. Season the salmon well with salt and freshly ground black pepper. Spray or brush the bottom of the air fryer basket with vegetable oil and place the salmon fillets inside. Air-fry the salmon for 5 minutes.

3. While the salmon is air-frying, combine the maple syrup, balsamic vinegar and Dijon mustard in a small saucepan over medium heat and stir to blend well. Let the mixture simmer while the fish is cooking. It should start to thicken slightly, but keep your eye on it so it doesn't burn.

4. Brush the glaze on the salmon fillets and air-fry for an additional 5 minutes. The salmon should feel firm to the touch when finished and the glaze should be nicely browned on top. Brush a little more glaze on top before removing and serving with rice and vegetables, or a nice green salad.

Tuna Patties With Dill Sauce

Servings: 6   Cooking Time: 10 Minutes

Ingredients:

- Two 5-ounce cans albacore tuna, drained
- ½ teaspoon garlic powder
- 2 teaspoons dried dill, divided
- ½ teaspoon black pepper
- ½ teaspoon salt, divided
- ¼ cup minced onion
- 1 large egg

- 7 tablespoons mayonnaise, divided
- ¼ cup panko breadcrumbs
- 1 teaspoon fresh lemon juice
- ¼ teaspoon fresh lemon zest
- 6 pieces butterleaf lettuce
- 1 cup diced tomatoes

Directions:

1. In a large bowl, mix the tuna with the garlic powder, 1 teaspoon of the dried dill, the black pepper, ¼ teaspoon of the salt, and the onion. Make sure to use the back of a fork to really break up the tuna so there are no large chunks.

2. Mix in the egg and 1 tablespoon of the mayonnaise; then fold in the breadcrumbs so the tuna begins to form a thick batter that holds together.

3. Portion the tuna mixture into 6 equal patties and place on a plate lined with parchment paper in the refrigerator for at least 30 minutes. This will help the patties hold together in the air fryer.

4. When ready to cook, preheat the air fryer to 350°F.

5. Liberally spray the metal trivet that sits inside the air fryer basket with olive oil mist and place the patties onto the trivet.

6. Cook for 5 minutes, flip, and cook another 5 minutes.

7. While the patties are cooking, make the dill sauce by combining the remaining 6 tablespoons of mayonnaise with the remaining 1 teaspoon of dill, the lemon juice, the lemon zest, and the remaining ¼ teaspoon of salt. Set aside.

8. Remove the patties from the air fryer.

9. Place 1 slice of lettuce on a plate and top with the tuna patty and a tomato slice. Repeat to form the remaining servings. Drizzle the dill dressing over the top. Serve immediately.

Sweet Potato–wrapped Shrimp

Servings:3

Cooking Time: 6 Minutes

Ingredients:

➢ 24 Long spiralized sweet potato strands

➢ Olive oil spray

➢ ¼ teaspoon Garlic powder

➢ ¼ teaspoon Table salt

➢ Up to a ⅛ teaspoon Cayenne

➢ 12 Large shrimp (20–25 per pound), peeled and deveined

Directions:

1. Preheat the air fryer to 400°F.

2. Lay the spiralized sweet potato strands on a large swath of paper towels and straighten out the strands to long ropes. Coat them with olive oil spray, then sprinkle them with the garlic powder, salt, and cayenne.

3. Pick up 2 strands and wrap them around the center of a shrimp, with the ends tucked under what now becomes the bottom side of the shrimp. Continue wrapping the remainder of the shrimp.

4. Set the shrimp bottom side down in the basket with as much air space between them as possible. Air-fry undisturbed for 6 minutes, or until the sweet potato strands are crisp and the shrimp are pink and firm.

5. Use kitchen tongs to transfer the shrimp to a wire rack. Cool for only a minute or two before serving.

Crab Cakes

Servings: 2

Cooking Time: 10 Minutes

Ingredients:

- 1 teaspoon butter
- ⅓ cup finely diced onion
- ⅓ cup finely diced celery
- ¼ cup mayonnaise
- 1 teaspoon Dijon mustard
- 1 egg
- pinch ground cayenne pepper
- 1 teaspoon salt
- freshly ground black pepper
- 16 ounces lump crabmeat
- ½ cup + 2 tablespoons panko breadcrumbs, divided

Directions:

1. Melt the butter in a skillet over medium heat. Sauté the onion and celery until it starts to soften, but not brown – about 4 minutes. Transfer the cooked vegetables to a large bowl. Add the mayonnaise, Dijon mustard, egg, cayenne pepper, salt and freshly ground black pepper to the bowl. Gently fold in the lump crabmeat and 2 tablespoons of panko breadcrumbs. Stir carefully so you don't break up all the crab pieces.

2. Preheat the air fryer to 400°F.

3. Place the remaining panko breadcrumbs in a shallow dish. Divide the crab mixture into 4 portions and shape each portion into a round patty. Dredge the crab patties in the breadcrumbs, coating both sides as well as the edges with the crumbs.

4. Air-fry the crab cakes for 5 minutes. Using a flat spatula, gently turn the cakes over and air-fry for another 5 minutes. Serve the crab cakes with tartar sauce or cocktail sauce, or dress it up with the suggestion below.

Five Spice Red Snapper With Green Onions And Orange Salsa

Servings: 2

Cooking Time: 8 Minutes

Ingredients:

- ➢ 2 oranges, peeled, segmented and chopped
- ➢ 1 tablespoon minced shallot
- ➢ 1 to 3 teaspoons minced red Jalapeño or Serrano pepper
- ➢ 1 tablespoon chopped fresh cilantro
- ➢ lime juice, to taste
- ➢ salt, to taste
- ➢ 2 (5- to 6-ounce) red snapper fillets
- ➢ ½ teaspoon Chinese five spice powder
- ➢ salt and freshly ground black pepper
- ➢ vegetable or olive oil, in a spray bottle
- ➢ 4 green onions, cut into 2-inch lengths

Directions:

1. Start by making the salsa. Cut the peel off the oranges, slicing around the oranges to expose the flesh. Segment the oranges by cutting in between the membranes of the orange. Chop the segments roughly and combine in a bowl with the shallot, Jalapeño or Serrano pepper, cilantro, lime juice and salt. Set the salsa aside.

2. Preheat the air fryer to 400°F.

3. Season the fish fillets with the five-spice powder, salt and freshly ground black pepper. Spray both sides of the fish fillets with oil. Toss the green onions with a little oil.

4. Transfer the fish to the air fryer basket and scatter the green onions around the fish. Air-fry at 400°F for 8 minutes.

5. Remove the fish from the air fryer, along with the fried green onions. Serve with white rice and a spoonful of the salsa on top.

Tex-mex Fish Tacos

Servings:3

Cooking Time: 7 Minutes

Ingredients:

➢ ¾ teaspoon Chile powder

➢ ¼ teaspoon Ground cumin

➢ ¼ teaspoon Dried oregano

➢ 3 5-ounce skinless mahi-mahi fillets

➢ Vegetable oil spray

➢ 3 Corn or flour tortillas

➢ 6 tablespoons Diced tomatoes

➢ 3 tablespoons Regular, low-fat, or fat-free sour cream

Directions:

1. Preheat the air fryer to 400°F.

2. Stir the chile powder, cumin, and oregano in a small bowl until well combined.

3. Coat each piece of fish all over (even the sides and ends) with vegetable oil spray. Sprinkle the spice mixture evenly over all sides of the fillets. Lightly spray them again.

4. When the machine is at temperature, set the fillets in the basket with as much air space between them as possible. Air-fry undisturbed for 7 minutes, until lightly browned and firm but not hard.

5. Use a nonstick-safe spatula to transfer the fillets to a wire rack. Microwave the tortillas on high for a few seconds, until supple. Put a fillet in each tortilla and top each with 2 tablespoons diced tomatoes and 1 tablespoon sour cream.

Italian Tuna Roast

Servings: 8

Cooking Time: 21 Minutes

Ingredients:

➤ cooking spray

➤ 1 tablespoon Italian seasoning

➤ ⅛ teaspoon ground black pepper

➤ 1 tablespoon extra-light olive oil

➤ 1 teaspoon lemon juice

➤ 1 tuna loin (approximately 2 pounds, 3 to 4 inches thick, large enough to fill a 6 x 6-inch baking dish)

Directions:

1. Spray baking dish with cooking spray and place in air fryer basket. Preheat air fryer to 390°F.

2. Mix together the Italian seasoning, pepper, oil, and lemon juice.

3. Using a dull table knife or butter knife, pierce top of tuna about every half inch: Insert knife into top of tuna roast and pierce almost all the way to the bottom.

4. Spoon oil mixture into each of the holes and use the knife to push seasonings into the tuna as deeply as possible.

5. Spread any remaining oil mixture on all outer surfaces of tuna.

6. Place tuna roast in baking dish and cook at 390°F for 20 minutes. Check temperature with a meat thermometer. Cook for an additional 1 minutes or until temperature reaches 145°F.

7. Remove basket from fryer and let tuna sit in basket for 10minutes.

Shrimp Teriyaki

Servings:10

Cooking Time: 6 Minutes

Ingredients:

➢ 1 tablespoon Regular or low-sodium soy sauce or gluten-free tamari sauce

➢ 1 tablespoon Mirin or a substitute (see here)

➢ 1 teaspoon Ginger juice (see the headnote)

➢ 10 Large shrimp (20–25 per pound), peeled and deveined

➢ ⅔ cup Plain panko bread crumbs (gluten-free, if a concern)

➢ 1 Large egg

➢ Vegetable oil spray

Directions:

1. Whisk the soy or tamari sauce, mirin, and ginger juice in an 8- or 9-inch square baking pan until uniform. Add the shrimp and toss well to coat. Cover and refrigerate for 1 hour, tossing the shrimp in the marinade at least twice.

2. Preheat the air fryer to 400°F.

3. Thread a marinated shrimp on a 4-inch bamboo skewer by inserting the pointy tip at the small end of the shrimp, then guiding the skewer along the shrimp so that the tip comes out the thick end and the shrimp is flat along the length of the skewer. Repeat with the remaining shrimp. (You'll need eight 4-inch skewers for the small batch, 10 skewers for the medium batch, and 12 for the large.)

4. Pour the bread crumbs onto a dinner plate. Whisk the egg in the baking pan with any marinade that stayed behind. Lay the skewers in the pan, in as close to a single layer as possible. Turn repeatedly to make sure the shrimp is coated in the egg mixture.

5. One at a time, take a skewered shrimp out of the pan and set it in the bread crumbs, turning several times and pressing gently until the shrimp is evenly coated on all sides. Coat the shrimp with vegetable oil spray and set the skewer aside. Repeat with the remainder of the shrimp.

6. Set the skewered shrimp in the basket in one layer. Air-fry undisturbed for 6 minutes, or until pink and firm.

7. Transfer the skewers to a wire rack. Cool for only a minute or two before serving.

Blackened Red Snapper

Servings: 4

Cooking Time: 8 Minutes

Ingredients:

- 1½ teaspoons black pepper
- ¼ teaspoon thyme
- ¼ teaspoon garlic powder
- ⅛ teaspoon cayenne pepper
- 1 teaspoon olive oil
- 4 4-ounce red snapper fillet portions, skin on
- 4 thin slices lemon
- cooking spray

Directions:

1. Mix the spices and oil together to make a paste. Rub into both sides of the fish.
2. Spray air fryer basket with nonstick cooking spray and lay snapper steaks in basket, skin-side down.
3. Place a lemon slice on each piece of fish.
4. Cook at 390°F for 8 minutes. The fish will not flake when done, but it should be white through the center.

POULTRY RECIPES

Jerk Chicken Drumsticks

Servings: 2

Cooking Time: 20 Minutes

Ingredients:

- ➢ 1 or 2 cloves garlic
- ➢ 1 inch of fresh ginger
- ➢ 2 serrano peppers, (with seeds if you like it spicy, seeds removed for less heat)
- ➢ 1 teaspoon ground allspice
- ➢ 1 teaspoon ground nutmeg
- ➢ 1 teaspoon chili powder
- ➢ ½ teaspoon dried thyme
- ➢ ½ teaspoon ground cinnamon
- ➢ ½ teaspoon paprika
- ➢ 1 tablespoon brown sugar
- ➢ 1 teaspoon soy sauce
- ➢ 2 tablespoons vegetable oil
- ➢ 6 skinless chicken drumsticks

Directions:

1. Combine all the ingredients except the chicken in a small chopper or blender and blend to a paste. Make slashes into the meat of the chicken drumsticks and rub the spice blend all over the chicken (a pair of plastic gloves makes this really easy). Transfer the rubbed chicken to a non-reactive covered container and let the chicken marinate for at least 30 minutes or overnight in the refrigerator.
2. Preheat the air fryer to 400°F.
3. Transfer the drumsticks to the air fryer basket. Air-fry for 10 minutes. Turn the drumsticks over and air-fry for another 10 minutes. Serve warm with some rice and vegetables or a green salad.

Lemon Sage Roast Chicken

Servings: 4

Cooking Time: 60 Minutes

Ingredients:

- ➤ 1 (4-pound) chicken
- ➤ 1 bunch sage, divided
- ➤ 1 lemon, zest and juice
- ➤ salt and freshly ground black pepper

Directions:

1. Preheat the air fryer to 350°F and pour a little water into the bottom of the air fryer drawer. (This will help prevent the grease that drips into the bottom drawer from burning and smoking.)

2. Run your fingers between the skin and flesh of the chicken breasts and thighs. Push a couple of sage leaves up underneath the skin of the chicken on each breast and each thigh.

3. Push some of the lemon zest up under the skin of the chicken next to the sage. Sprinkle some of the zest inside the chicken cavity, and reserve any leftover zest. Squeeze the lemon juice all over the chicken and in the cavity as well.

4. Season the chicken, inside and out, with the salt and freshly ground black pepper. Set a few sage leaves aside for the final garnish. Crumple up the remaining sage leaves and push them into the cavity of the chicken, along with one of the squeezed lemon halves.

5. Place the chicken breast side up into the air fryer basket and air-fry for 20 minutes at 350°F. Flip the chicken over so that it is breast side down and continue to air-fry for another 20 minutes. Return the chicken to breast side up and finish air-frying for 20 more minutes. The internal temperature of the chicken should register 165°F in the thickest part of the thigh when fully cooked. Remove the chicken from the air fryer and let it rest on a cutting board for at least 5 minutes.

6. Cut the rested chicken into pieces, sprinkle with the reserved lemon zest and garnish with the reserved sage leaves.

Coconut Chicken With Apricot-ginger Sauce

Servings: 4   Cooking Time: 8 Minutes Per Batch

Ingredients:

- 1½ pounds boneless, skinless chicken tenders, cut in large chunks (about 1¼ inches)
- salt and pepper
- ½ cup cornstarch
- 2 eggs
- 1 tablespoon milk
- 3 cups shredded coconut (see below)
- oil for misting or cooking spray
- Apricot-Ginger Sauce
- ½ cup apricot preserves
- 2 tablespoons white vinegar
- ¼ teaspoon ground ginger
- ¼ teaspoon low-sodium soy sauce
- 2 teaspoons white or yellow onion, grated or finely minced

Directions:

1. Mix all ingredients for the Apricot-Ginger Sauce well and let sit for flavors to blend while you cook the chicken.

2. Season chicken chunks with salt and pepper to taste.

3. Place cornstarch in a shallow dish.

4. In another shallow dish, beat together eggs and milk.

5. Place coconut in a third shallow dish. (If also using panko breadcrumbs, as suggested below, stir them to mix well.)

6. Spray air fryer basket with oil or cooking spray.

7. Dip each chicken chunk into cornstarch, shake off excess, and dip in egg mixture.

8. Shake off excess egg mixture and roll lightly in coconut or coconut mixture. Spray with oil.

9. Place coated chicken chunks in air fryer basket in a single layer, close together but without sides touching.

10. Cook at 360°F for 4minutes, stop, and turn chunks over.

11. Cook an additional 4 minutes or until chicken is done inside and coating is crispy brown.

12. Repeat steps 9 through 11 to cook remaining chicken chunks.

Jerk Turkey Meatballs

Servings: 7   Cooking Time: 8 Minutes

Ingredients:

- 1 pound lean ground turkey
- ¼ cup chopped onion
- 1 teaspoon minced garlic
- ½ teaspoon dried thyme
- ¼ teaspoon ground cinnamon
- 1 teaspoon cayenne pepper
- ½ teaspoon paprika
- ½ teaspoon salt
- ⅛ teaspoon black pepper
- ¼ teaspoon red pepper flakes
- 2 teaspoons brown sugar
- 1 large egg, whisked
- ⅓ cup panko breadcrumbs
- 2⅓ cups cooked brown Jasmine rice
- 2 green onions, chopped
- ¾ cup sweet onion dressing

Directions:

1. Preheat the air fryer to 350°F.

2. In a medium bowl, mix the ground turkey with the onion, garlic, thyme, cinnamon, cayenne pepper, paprika, salt, pepper, red pepper flakes, and brown sugar. Add the whisked egg and stir in the breadcrumbs until the turkey starts to hold together.

3. Using a 1-ounce scoop, portion the turkey into meatballs. You should get about 28 meatballs.

4. Spray the air fryer basket with olive oil spray.

5. Place the meatballs into the air fryer basket and cook for 5 minutes, shake the basket, and cook another 2 to 4 minutes (or until the internal temperature of the meatballs reaches 165°F).

6. Remove the meatballs from the basket and repeat for the remaining meatballs.

7. Serve warm over a bed of rice with chopped green onions and spicy Caribbean jerk dressing.

Italian Roasted Chicken Thighs

Servings: 6

Cooking Time: 14 Minutes

Ingredients:

➢ 6 boneless chicken thighs

➢ ½ teaspoon dried oregano

➢ ½ teaspoon garlic powder

➢ ½ teaspoon sea salt

➢ ½ teaspoon black pepper

➢ ¼ teaspoon crushed red pepper flakes

Directions:

1. Pat the chicken thighs with paper towel.

2. In a small bowl, mix the oregano, garlic powder, salt, pepper, and crushed red pepper flakes. Rub the spice mixture onto the chicken thighs.

3. Preheat the air fryer to 400°F.

4. Place the chicken thighs in the air fryer basket and spray with cooking spray. Cook for 10 minutes, turn over, and cook another 4 minutes. When cooking completes, the internal temperature should read 165°F.

Maple Bacon Wrapped Chicken Breasts

Servings: 2

Cooking Time: 18 Minutes

Ingredients:

- 2 (6-ounce) boneless, skinless chicken breasts
- 2 tablespoons maple syrup, divided
- freshly ground black pepper
- 6 slices thick-sliced bacon
- fresh celery or parsley leaves
- Ranch Dressing:
- ¼ cup mayonnaise
- ¼ cup buttermilk
- ¼ cup Greek yogurt
- 1 tablespoon chopped fresh chives
- 1 tablespoon chopped fresh parsley
- 1 tablespoon chopped fresh dill
- 1 tablespoon lemon juice
- salt and freshly ground black pepper

Directions:

1. Brush the chicken breasts with half the maple syrup and season with freshly ground black pepper. Wrap three slices of bacon around each chicken breast, securing the ends with toothpicks.

2. Preheat the air fryer to 380°F.

3. Air-fry the chicken for 6 minutes. Then turn the chicken breasts over, pour more maple syrup on top and air-fry for another 6 minutes. Turn the chicken breasts one more time, brush the remaining maple syrup all over and continue to air-fry for a final 6 minutes.

4. While the chicken is cooking, prepare the dressing by combining all the dressing ingredients together in a bowl.

5. When the chicken has finished cooking, remove the toothpicks and serve each breast with a little dressing drizzled over each one. Scatter lots of fresh celery or parsley leaves on top.

Crispy "fried" Chicken

Servings: 4

Cooking Time: 14 Minutes

Ingredients:

➢ ¾ cup all-purpose flour
➢ ½ teaspoon paprika
➢ ¼ teaspoon black pepper
➢ ¼ teaspoon salt
➢ 2 large eggs
➢ 1½ cups panko breadcrumbs
➢ 1 pound boneless, skinless chicken tenders

Directions:

1. Preheat the air fryer to 400°F.
2. In a shallow bowl, mix the flour with the paprika, pepper, and salt.
3. In a separate bowl, whisk the eggs; set aside.
4. In a third bowl, place the breadcrumbs.
5. Liberally spray the air fryer basket with olive oil spray.
6. Pat the chicken tenders dry with a paper towel. Dredge the tenders one at a time in the flour, then dip them in the egg, and toss them in the breadcrumb coating. Repeat until all tenders are coated.
7. Set each tender in the air fryer, leaving room on each side of the tender to allow for flipping.
8. When the basket is full, cook 4 to 7 minutes, flip, and cook another 4 to 7 minutes.
9. Remove the tenders and let cool 5 minutes before serving. Repeat until all tenders are cooked.

Quick Chicken For Filling

Servings: 2

Cooking Time: 8 Minutes

Ingredients:

➤ 1 pound chicken tenders, skinless and boneless

➤ ½ teaspoon ground cumin

➤ ½ teaspoon garlic powder

➤ cooking spray

Directions:

1. Sprinkle raw chicken tenders with seasonings.

2. Spray air fryer basket lightly with cooking spray to prevent sticking.

3. Place chicken in air fryer basket in single layer.

4. Cook at 390°F for 4minutes, turn chicken strips over, and cook for an additional 4minutes.

5. Test for doneness. Thick tenders may require an additional minute or two.

Philly Chicken Cheesesteak Stromboli

Servings: 2   Cooking Time: 28 Minutes

Ingredients:

➤ ½ onion, sliced

➤ 1 teaspoon vegetable oil

➤ 2 boneless, skinless chicken breasts, partially frozen and sliced very thin on the bias (about 1 pound)

➤ 1 tablespoon Worcestershire sauce

➤ salt and freshly ground black pepper

➤ ½ recipe of Blue Jean Chef pizza dough (see page 229), or 14 ounces of store-bought pizza dough

➤ 1½ cups grated Cheddar cheese

➤ ½ cup Cheese Whiz® (or other jarred cheese sauce), warmed gently in the microwave

➤ tomato ketchup for serving

Directions:

1. Preheat the air fryer to 400°F.

2. Toss the sliced onion with oil and air-fry for 8 minutes, stirring halfway through the cooking time. Add the sliced chicken and Worcestershire sauce to the air fryer basket, and toss to evenly distribute the ingredients. Season the mixture with salt and freshly ground black pepper and air-fry for 8 minutes, stirring a couple of times during the cooking process. Remove the chicken and onion from the air fryer and let the mixture cool a little.

3. On a lightly floured surface, roll or press the pizza dough out into a 13-inch by 11-inch rectangle, with the long side closest to you. Sprinkle half of the Cheddar cheese over the dough leaving an empty 1-inch border from the edge farthest away from you. Top the cheese with the chicken and onion mixture, spreading it out evenly. Drizzle the cheese sauce over the meat and sprinkle the remaining Cheddar cheese on top.

4. Start rolling the stromboli away from you and toward the empty border. Make sure the filling stays tightly tucked inside the roll. Finally, tuck the ends of the dough in and pinch the seam shut. Place the seam side down and shape the Stromboli into a U-shape to fit in the air-fry basket. Cut 4 small slits with the tip of a sharp knife evenly in the top of the dough and lightly brush the stromboli with a little oil.

5. Preheat the air fryer to 370°F.

6. Spray or brush the air fryer basket with oil and transfer the U-shaped stromboli to the air fryer basket. Air-fry for 12 minutes, turning the stromboli over halfway through the cooking time. (Use a plate to invert the stromboli out of the air fryer basket and then slide it back into the basket off the plate.)

7. To remove, carefully flip stromboli over onto a cutting board. Let it rest for a couple of minutes before serving. Slice the stromboli into 3-inch pieces and serve with ketchup for dipping, if desired.

Crispy Chicken Parmesan

Servings: 4

Cooking Time: 12 Minutes

Ingredients:

- ➤ 4 skinless, boneless chicken breasts, pounded thin to ¼-inch thickness
- ➤ 1 teaspoon salt, divided
- ➤ ½ teaspoon black pepper, divided
- ➤ 1 cup flour
- ➤ 2 eggs
- ➤ 1 cup panko breadcrumbs
- ➤ ½ teaspoon dried oregano
- ➤ ½ cup grated Parmesan cheese

Directions:

1. Pat the chicken breasts with a paper towel. Season the chicken with ½ teaspoon of the salt and ¼ teaspoon of the pepper.

2. In a medium bowl, place the flour.

3. In a second bowl, whisk the eggs.

4. In a third bowl, place the breadcrumbs, oregano, cheese, and the remaining ½ teaspoon of salt and ¼ teaspoon of pepper.

5. Dredge the chicken in the flour and shake off the excess. Dip the chicken into the eggs and then into the breadcrumbs. Set the chicken on a plate and repeat with the remaining chicken pieces.

6. Preheat the air fryer to 360°F.

7. Place the chicken in the air fryer basket and spray liberally with cooking spray. Cook for 8 minutes, turn the chicken breasts over, and cook another 4 minutes. When golden brown, check for an internal temperature of 165°F.

Simple Buttermilk Fried Chicken

Servings: 4

Cooking Time: 27 Minutes

Ingredients:

- ➤ 1 (4-pound) chicken, cut into 8 pieces
- ➤ 2 cups buttermilk
- ➤ hot sauce (optional)
- ➤ 1½ cups flour*
- ➤ 2 teaspoons paprika
- ➤ 1 teaspoon salt
- ➤ freshly ground black pepper
- ➤ 2 eggs, lightly beaten
- ➤ vegetable oil, in a spray bottle

Directions:

1. Cut the chicken into 8 pieces and submerge them in the buttermilk and hot sauce, if using. A zipper-sealable plastic bag works well for this. Let the chicken soak in the buttermilk for at least one hour or even overnight in the refrigerator.

2. Set up a dredging station. Mix the flour, paprika, salt and black pepper in a clean zipper-sealable plastic bag. Whisk the eggs and place them in a shallow dish. Remove four pieces of chicken from the buttermilk and transfer them to the bag with the flour. Shake them around to coat on all sides. Remove the chicken from the flour, shaking off any excess flour, and dip them into the beaten egg. Return the chicken to the bag of seasoned flour and shake again. Set the coated chicken aside and repeat with the remaining four pieces of chicken.

3. Preheat the air fryer to 370°F.

4. Spray the chicken on all sides with the vegetable oil and then transfer one batch to the air fryer basket. Air-fry the chicken at 370°F for 20 minutes, flipping the pieces over halfway through the cooking process, taking care not to knock off the breading. Transfer the chicken to a plate, but do not cover. Repeat with the second batch of chicken.

5. Lower the temperature on the air fryer to 340°F. Flip the chicken back over and place the first batch of chicken on top of the second batch already in the basket. Air-fry for another 7 minutes and serve warm.

Pickle Brined Fried Chicken

Servings: 4   Cooking Time: 47 Minutes

Ingredients:

- 4 bone-in, skin-on chicken legs, cut into drumsticks and thighs (about 3½ pounds)
- pickle juice from a 24-ounce jar of kosher dill pickles
- ½ cup flour
- salt and freshly ground black pepper
- 2 eggs

- 1 cup fine breadcrumbs
- 1 teaspoon salt
- 1 teaspoon freshly ground black pepper
- ½ teaspoon ground paprika
- ⅛ teaspoon ground cayenne pepper
- vegetable or canola oil in a spray bottle

Directions:

1. Place the chicken in a shallow dish and pour the pickle juice over the top. Cover and transfer the chicken to the refrigerator to brine in the pickle juice for 3 to 8 hours.

2. When you are ready to cook, remove the chicken from the refrigerator to let it come to room temperature while you set up a dredging station. Place the flour in a shallow dish and season well with salt and freshly ground black pepper. Whisk the eggs in a second shallow dish. In a third shallow dish, combine the breadcrumbs, salt, pepper, paprika and cayenne pepper.

3. Preheat the air fryer to 370°F.

4. Remove the chicken from the pickle brine and gently dry it with a clean kitchen towel. Dredge each piece of chicken in the flour, then dip it into the egg mixture, and finally press it into the breadcrumb mixture to coat all sides of the chicken. Place the breaded chicken on a plate or baking sheet and spray each piece all over with vegetable oil.

5. Air-fry the chicken in two batches. Place two chicken thighs and two drumsticks into the air fryer basket. Air-fry for 10 minutes. Then, gently turn the chicken pieces over and air-fry for another 10 minutes. Remove the chicken pieces and let them rest on plate – do not cover. Repeat with the second batch of chicken, air-frying for 20 minutes, turning the chicken over halfway through.

6. Lower the temperature of the air fryer to 340°F. Place the first batch of chicken on top of the second batch already in the basket and air-fry for an additional 7 minutes. Serve warm and enjoy.

DESSERTS AND SWEETS

Glazed Cherry Turnovers

Servings: 8

Cooking Time: 14 Minutes

Ingredients:

➢ 2 sheets frozen puff pastry, thawed

➢ 1 (21-ounce) can premium cherry pie filling

➢ 2 teaspoons ground cinnamon

➢ 1 egg, beaten

➢ 1 cup sliced almonds

➢ 1 cup powdered sugar

➢ 2 tablespoons milk

Directions:

1. Roll a sheet of puff pastry out into a square that is approximately 10-inches by 10-inches. Cut this large square into quarters.

2. Mix the cherry pie filling and cinnamon together in a bowl. Spoon ¼ cup of the cherry filling into the center of each puff pastry square. Brush the perimeter of the pastry square with the egg wash. Fold one corner of the puff pastry over the cherry pie filling towards the opposite corner, forming a triangle. Seal the two edges of the pastry together with the tip of a fork, making a design with the tines. Brush the top of the turnovers with the egg wash and sprinkle sliced almonds over each one. Repeat these steps with the second sheet of puff pastry. You should have eight turnovers at the end.

3. Preheat the air fryer to 370°F.

4. Air-fry two turnovers at a time for 14 minutes, carefully turning them over halfway through the cooking time.

5. While the turnovers are cooking, make the glaze by whisking the powdered sugar and milk together in a small bowl until smooth. Let the glaze sit for a minute so the sugar can absorb the milk. If the consistency is still too thick to drizzle, add a little more milk, a drop at a time, and stir until smooth.

6. Let the cooked cherry turnovers sit for at least 10 minutes. Then drizzle the glaze over each turnover in a zigzag motion. Serve warm or at room temperature.

Caramel Apple Crumble

Servings: 6

Cooking Time: 50 Minutes

Ingredients:

- ➤ 4 apples, peeled and thinly sliced
- ➤ 2 tablespoons sugar
- ➤ 1 tablespoon flour
- ➤ 1 teaspoon ground cinnamon
- ➤ ¼ teaspoon ground allspice
- ➤ healthy pinch ground nutmeg
- ➤ 10 caramel squares, cut into small pieces
- ➤ Crumble Topping:
- ➤ ¾ cup rolled oats
- ➤ ¼ cup sugar
- ➤ ⅓ cup flour
- ➤ ¼ teaspoon ground cinnamon
- ➤ 6 tablespoons butter, melted

Directions:

1. Preheat the air fryer to 330°F.

2. Combine the apples, sugar, flour, and spices in a large bowl and toss to coat. Add the caramel pieces and mix well. Pour the apple mixture into a 1-quart round baking dish that will fit in your air fryer basket (6-inch diameter).

3. To make the crumble topping, combine the rolled oats, sugar, flour and cinnamon in a small bowl. Add the melted butter and mix well. Top the apples with the crumble mixture. Cover the entire dish with aluminum foil and transfer the dish to the air fryer basket, lowering the dish into the basket using a sling made of aluminum foil (fold a piece of aluminum foil into a strip about 2-inches wide by 24-inches long). Fold the ends of the aluminum foil over the top of the dish before returning the basket to the air fryer.

4. Air-fry at 330°F for 25 minutes. Remove the aluminum foil and continue to air-fry for another 25 minutes. Serve the crumble warm with whipped cream or vanilla ice cream, if desired.

Puff Pastry Apples

Servings: 4   Cooking Time: 10 Minutes

Ingredients:

- ➢ 3 Rome or Gala apples, peeled
- ➢ 2 tablespoons sugar
- ➢ 1 teaspoon all-purpose flour
- ➢ 1 teaspoon ground cinnamon
- ➢ ⅛ teaspoon ground ginger
- ➢ pinch ground nutmeg

- ➢ 1 sheet puff pastry
- ➢ 1 tablespoon butter, cut into 4 pieces
- ➢ 1 egg, beaten
- ➢ vegetable oil
- ➢ vanilla ice cream (optional)
- ➢ caramel sauce (optional)

Directions:

1. Remove the core from the apple by cutting the four sides off the apple around the core. Slice the pieces of apple into thin half-moons, about ¼-inch thick. Combine the sugar, flour, cinnamon, ginger, and nutmeg in a large bowl. Add the apples to the bowl and gently toss until the apples are evenly coated with the spice mixture. Set aside.

2. Cut the puff pastry sheet into a 12-inch by 12-inch square. Then quarter the sheet into four 6-inch squares. Save any remaining pastry for decorating the apples at the end.

3. Divide the spiced apples between the four puff pastry squares, stacking the apples in the center of each square and placing them flat on top of each other in a circle. Top the apples with a piece of the butter.

4. Brush the four edges of the pastry with the egg wash. Bring the four corners of the pastry together, wrapping them around the apple slices and pinching them together at the top in the style of a "beggars purse" appetizer. Fold the ends of the pastry corners down onto the apple making them look like leaves. Brush the entire apple with the egg wash.

5. Using the leftover dough, make leaves to decorate the apples. Cut out 8 leaf shapes, about 1½-inches long, "drawing" the leaf veins on the pastry leaves with a paring knife. Place 2 leaves on the top of each apple, tucking the ends of the leaves under the pastry in the center of the apples. Brush the top of the leaves with additional egg wash. Sprinkle the entire apple with some granulated sugar.

6. Preheat the air fryer to 350°F.

7. Spray or brush the inside of the air fryer basket with oil. Place the apples in the basket and air-fry for 6 minutes. Carefully turn the apples over – it's easiest to remove one apple, then flip the others over and finally return the last apple to the air fryer. Air-fry for an additional 4 minutes.

8. Serve the puff pastry apples warm with vanilla ice cream and drizzle with some caramel sauce.

Cherry Hand Pies

Servings: 8

Cooking Time: 8 Minutes

Ingredients:

➢ 4 cups frozen or canned pitted tart cherries (if using canned, drain and pat dry)

➢ 2 teaspoons lemon juice

➢ ½ cup sugar

➢ ¼ cup cornstarch

➢ 1 teaspoon vanilla extract

➢ 1 Basic Pie Dough (see the preceding recipe) or store-bought pie dough

Directions:

1. In a medium saucepan, place the cherries and lemon juice and cook over medium heat for 10 minutes, or until the cherries begin to break down.

2. In a small bowl, stir together the sugar and cornstarch. Pour the sugar mixture into the cherries, stirring constantly. Cook the cherry mixture over low heat for 2 to 3 minutes, or until thickened. Remove from the heat and stir in the vanilla extract. Allow the cherry mixture to cool to room temperature, about 30 minutes.

3. Meanwhile, bring the pie dough to room temperature. Divide the dough into 8 equal pieces. Roll out the dough to ¼-inch thickness in circles. Place ¼ cup filling in the center of each rolled dough. Fold the dough to create a half-circle. Using a fork, press around the edges to seal the hand pies. Pierce the top of the pie with a fork for steam release while cooking. Continue until 8 hand pies are formed.

4. Preheat the air fryer to 350°F.

5. Place a single layer of hand pies in the air fryer basket and spray with cooking spray. Cook for 8 to 10 minutes or until golden brown and cooked through.

Sweet Potato Pie Rolls

Servings:3

Cooking Time: 8 Minutes

Ingredients:

➢ 6 Spring roll wrappers

➢ 1½ cups Canned yams in syrup, drained

➢ 2 tablespoons Light brown sugar

➢ ¼ teaspoon Ground cinnamon

➢ 1 Large egg(s), well beaten

➢ Vegetable oil spray

Directions:

1. Preheat the air fryer to 400°F.

2. Set a spring roll wrapper on a clean, dry work surface. Scoop up ¼ cup of the pulpy yams and set along one edge of the wrapper, leaving 2 inches on each side of the yams. Top the yams with about 1 teaspoon brown sugar and a pinch of ground cinnamon. Fold the sides of the wrapper perpendicular to the yam filling up and over the filling, partially covering it. Brush beaten egg(s) over the side of the wrapper farthest from the yam. Starting with the yam end, roll the wrapper closed, ending at the part with the beaten egg that you can press gently to seal. Lightly coat the roll on all sides with vegetable oil spray. Set it aside seam side down and continue filling, rolling, and spraying the remaining wrappers in the same way.

3. Set the rolls seam side down in the basket with as much air space between them as possible. Air-fry undisturbed for 8 minutes, or until crisp and golden brown.

4. Use a nonstick-safe spatula and perhaps kitchen tongs for balance to gently transfer the rolls to a wire rack. Cool for at least 5 minutes or up to 30 minutes before serving.

Roasted Pears

Servings: 4

Cooking Time: 10 Minutes

Ingredients:

➢ 2 Ripe pears, preferably Anjou, stemmed, peeled, halved lengthwise, and cored

➢ 2 tablespoons Butter, melted

➢ 2 teaspoons Granulated white sugar

➢ Grated nutmeg

➢ ¼ cup Honey

➢ ½ cup (about 1½ ounces) Shaved Parmesan cheese

Directions:

1. Preheat the air fryer to 400°F.

2. Brush each pear half with about 1½ teaspoons of the melted butter, then sprinkle their cut sides with ½ teaspoon sugar. Grate a pinch of nutmeg over each pear.

3. When the machine is at temperature, set the pear halves cut side up in the basket with as much air space between them as possible. Air-fry undisturbed for 10 minutes, or until hot and softened.

4. Use a nonstick-safe spatula, and perhaps a flatware tablespoon for balance, to transfer the pear halves to a serving platter or plates. Cool for a minute or two, then drizzle each pear half with 1 tablespoon of the honey. Lay about 2 tablespoons of shaved Parmesan over each half just before serving.

Chocolate Cake

Servings: 8

Cooking Time: 20 Minutes

Ingredients:

➢ ½ cup sugar

➢ ¼ cup flour, plus 3 tablespoons

➢ 3 tablespoons cocoa

➢ ½ teaspoon baking powder

➢ ½ teaspoon baking soda

➢ ¼ teaspoon salt

➢ 1 egg

➢ 2 tablespoons oil

➢ ½ cup milk

➢ ½ teaspoon vanilla extract

Directions:

1. Preheat air fryer to 330°F.

2. Grease and flour a 6 x 6-inch baking pan.

3. In a medium bowl, stir together the sugar, flour, cocoa, baking powder, baking soda, and salt.

4. Add all other ingredients and beat with a wire whisk until smooth.

5. Pour batter into prepared pan and bake at 330°F for 20 minutes, until toothpick inserted in center comes out clean or with crumbs clinging to it.

Fried Snickers Bars

Servings:8

Cooking Time: 4 Minutes

Ingredients:

➢ ⅓ cup All-purpose flour

➢ 1 Large egg white(s), beaten until foamy

➢ 1½ cups (6 ounces) Vanilla wafer cookie crumbs

➢ 8 Fun-size (0.6-ounce/17-gram) Snickers bars, frozen

➢ Vegetable oil spray

Directions:

1. Preheat the air fryer to 400°F.

2. Set up and fill three shallow soup plates or small pie plates on your counter: one for the flour, one for the beaten egg white(s), and one for the cookie crumbs.

3. Unwrap the frozen candy bars. Dip one in the flour, turning it to coat on all sides. Gently shake off any excess, then set it in the beaten egg white(s). Turn it to coat all sides, even the ends, then let any excess egg white slip back into the rest. Set the candy bar in the cookie crumbs. Turn to coat on all sides, even the ends. Dip the candy bar back in the egg white(s) a second time, then into the cookie crumbs a second time, making sure you have an even coating all around. Coat the covered candy bar all over with vegetable oil spray. Set aside so you can dip and coat the remaining candy bars.

4. Set the coated candy bars in the basket with as much air space between them as possible. Air-fry undisturbed for 4 minutes, or until golden brown.

5. Remove the basket from the machine and let the candy bars cool in the basket for 10 minutes. Use a nonstick-safe spatula to transfer them to a wire rack and cool for 5 minutes more before chowing down.

Maple Cinnamon Cheesecake

Servings: 4

Cooking Time: 12 Minutes

Ingredients:

➤ 6 sheets of cinnamon graham crackers

➤ 2 tablespoons butter

➤ 8 ounces Neufchâtel cream cheese

➤ 3 tablespoons pure maple syrup

➤ 1 large egg

➤ ½ teaspoon ground cinnamon

➤ ¼ teaspoon salt

Directions:

1. Preheat the air fryer to 350°F.

2. Place the graham crackers in a food processor and process until crushed into a flour. Mix with the butter and press into a mini air-fryer-safe pan lined at the bottom with parchment paper. Place in the air fryer and cook for 4 minutes.

3. In a large bowl, place the cream cheese and maple syrup. Use a hand mixer or stand mixer and beat together until smooth. Add in the egg, cinnamon, and salt and mix on medium speed until combined.

4. Remove the graham cracker crust from the air fryer and pour the batter into the pan.

5. Place the pan back in the air fryer, adjusting the temperature to 315°F. Cook for 18 minutes. Carefully remove when cooking completes. The top should be lightly browned and firm.

6. Keep the cheesecake in the pan and place in the refrigerator for 3 or more hours to firm up before serving.

CPSIA information can be obtained
at www.ICGtesting.com
Printed in the USA
BVHW050748190122
626602BV00003B/198